Praise for the book

The marvellous tale of Salhesh is a Dalit attempt to humanize the wretched soul of a civilization haunted by caste and and vacuous empathy. To embody the good of humanity, Sahlesh has to be reborn a Dalit, a Dusadh of the great Himalayan lineage. This story brings to bear the moral–philosophical manifesto that every ruler who renounces power and serves humanity attains nobility. Kings have come and gone, but those like Ashoka and Sahlesh live on. Martine Le Coz offers us this treasure of a tale by placing her ear to Urmila Devi's heart. *The King of the Mountain* is Dalit.

Suraj Yengde
author of *Caste Matters*

Imagine a world filled with magic, redolent with the immanence of the divine, where an epiphany could emerge from the shadow of any rock, where women hold the truest secrets of life, where spiritual knowledge exists in the whisper of the wind, in the teachings of ragged old men, where the impulse of equality is innate and not learned… Martine Le Coz enters such a world, one created and inhabited by the Dalit Dusadh people of the Mithila region. Through the story of Salhesh, the prince who rejects his ruling caste destiny and chooses to be reborn through a Dalit womb, she leads us into a shimmering labyrinth of ontology, ethics and metaphysics. *The King of the Mountain* brings us face to face with the fact that the most profound insights of Indic culture have always lain with the marginalized who speak in voices that we have chosen not to hear. Listen now, before it is too late.

Arshia Sattar
translator of Valmiki's *Ramayana*

At each turn, *The King of the Mountain* reminded me that there are stories that are excised from memory because their inherent power frightens those who devise myth and record history. At each turn, *The King of the Mountain* gave me a story of a bevy of protagonists, that soothed me with the salve of hope—something it did for the Dusadhs of Madhubani for well over a millennium. A story more vital than ever now, in this age of manufactured fractures and enmities. Here, the king, Salhesh, *chooses* to be reborn to a Dalit midwife, he chooses to lead all living beings into a community untainted by caste or gender or species divisions. He chooses to renounce war, and then chooses a woman, a woman considered untouchable, as his heir. This is an epic story that we need to hear, that we need to tell, sing and celebrate. This is a story to remind us that equality and justice and oneness with the larger, non-human world, are not imports, nor recent ideas: outliers they may be, but they are part of an intrinsic, undying tradition of the land.

Karthika Naïr
author of *Until the Lions: Echoes from the Mahabharata*

The print medium is usually regarded as an instrument of democratization. Ironically, it has worked in reverse as far as India's epic narratives, the *Ramayana* and the *Mahabharata*, are concerned. Although these epics have been nourished for centuries through the 'tellings', in A.K. Ramanujan's phrase, of varied subaltern caste groups, the selective mechanism of the printed critical edition has ensured their strong identification with the casteist values and patriarchal interests of the savarna elites. By contrast, *The King of the Mountain* comes as a breath of fresh air. It is a Dalit epic, a legend of the marginalized Dusadh/Paswan community in northern Bihar, and tells of King Salhesh, a Kshatriya who willingly gives up his privileges to be reborn in a disadvantaged ethos. Strongly imbued with Buddhist values, this legend emphasizes solidarity and compassion, the interrelationships between humankind and other species, and the balance between the masculine and feminine aspects of the self. Drawing on many versions of the epic—as song, performance and visual art—Martine Le Coz has composed a narrative that redefines what it means to be truly heroic. *The King of the Mountain* is a vital contribution in an epoch dominated by the cult of the strongman, the hegemon and the tyrant.

Ranjit Hoskote
poet, translator and cultural theorist

THE KING OF THE MOUNTAIN

Martine Le Coz

Translated from the French by
REGAN KRAMER

navayana

The King of the Mountain: The Saga of King Salhesh
Martine Le Coz
Translated from the French by Regan Kramer
Published as *Le roi de la montagne* by Massot Editions, 2019
Hardback ISBN 9788194865476

First published in English, January 2022

The work is published with the support of the Publication Assistance Programmes of the Institut Français.

PAP
TAGORE

All rights reserved. No part of this book may be reproduced, stored in a retrieval system, or transmitted in any form or by any means, electronic, mechanical, photocopying, recording or otherwise, without the prior permission of the publisher.

Navayana Publishing Pvt Ltd
155 2nd Floor
Shahpur Jat, New Delhi 110049
Phone: +91-11-26494795
navayana.org

Typeset at Navayana

Printed by Sanjiv Palliwal, New Delhi

Distributed in South Asia by HarperCollins India

Subscribe to updates at navayana.org/subscribe
Follow on facebook.com/Navayana

To Urmila Devi
and the children of the Mountain

Map of India, seventh century

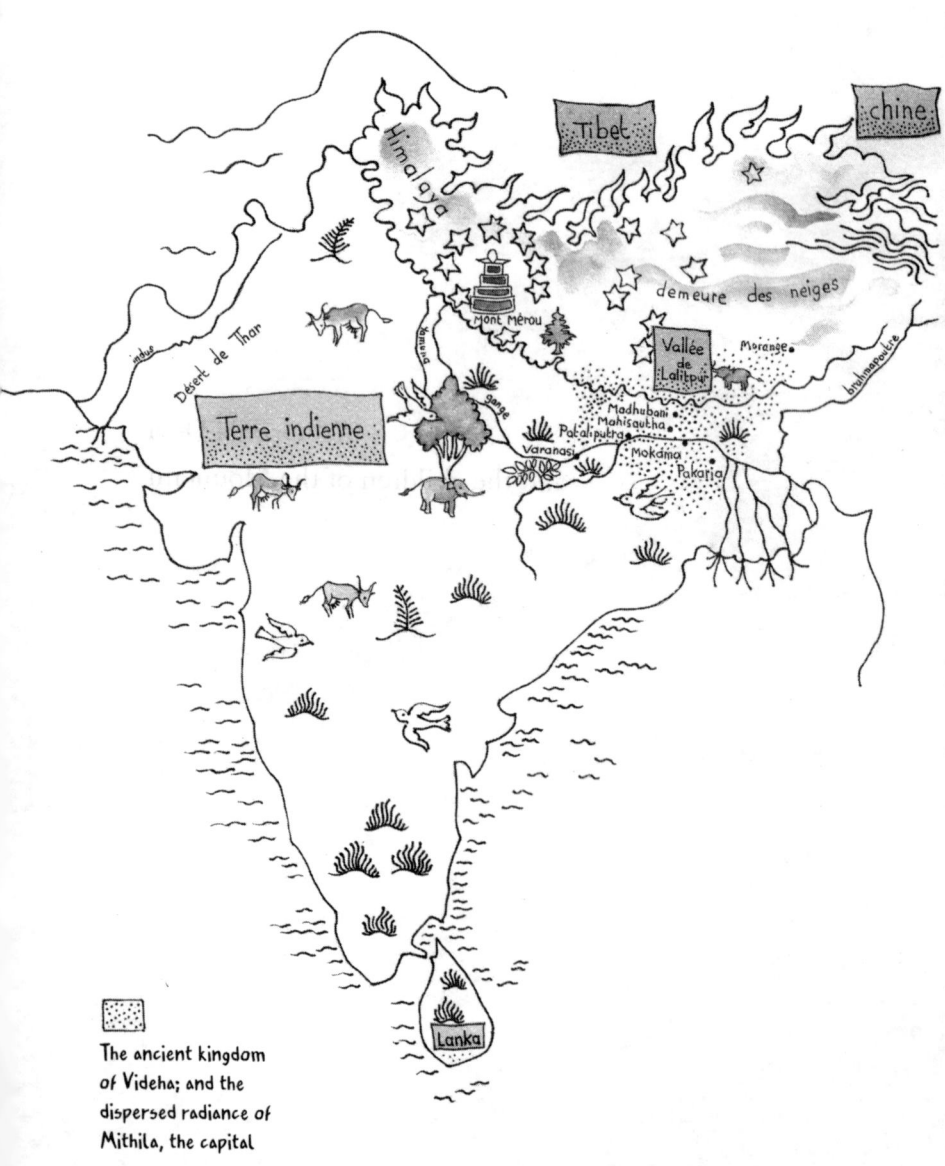

The ancient kingdom of Videha; and the dispersed radiance of Mithila, the capital

Drawings by Martine Le Coz

Genealogical tree of Salhesh

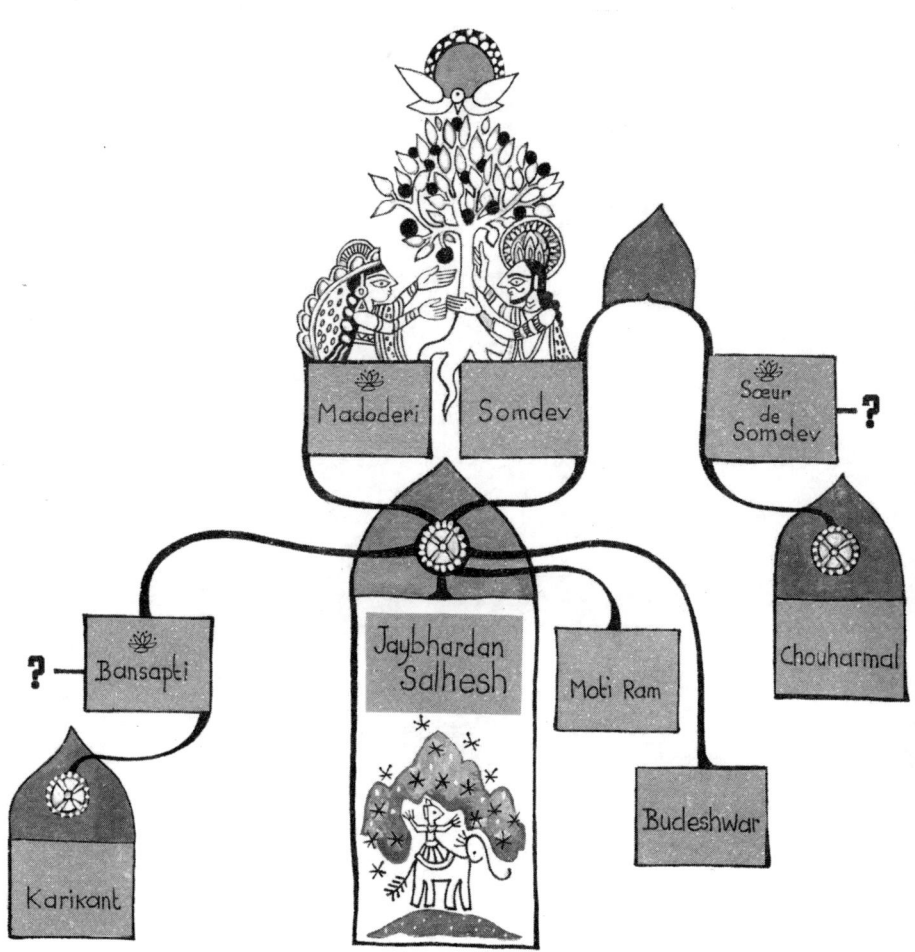

Map, tree	10
The King of the Mountain	15
Afterword 'The Saga of King Salhesh'	219
Outroduction: A Triangle Marked by a Dot	235
About the author and translator	252

1

1

Far in the distance, dawn came trickling down the Mountain, streaking the forest with orange, unfurling yellow butterflies from under the shoulders of trees. Their venerable arms raised to the sky, the trees proclaimed their age and patience to the firmament. The gods ruled in the remains of the night. None could hear what stories the wind told, but deep within the bark, in the thickness of their resin, in their seeds and fruits, the trees bore the groans and chants of an ancient battle.

Several kingdoms crowded together on a plain swept by the humid exhalations of Bengal. The wild beasts preferred the moist, tangled jungles, but the serpents poured their mirror-scaled bodies without discrimination, forming indecipherable messages in the undergrowth. Swollen with dreams, the rivers harassed the land. Wishing to seduce and ravish the Mountain, they pushed up against its belly.

On their glistening surface passed reflections, of a horse with seven mouths, a wondrous cow with four udders, and images of a paradise to set the deodars groaning. Demon drums reverberated in their depths. Their waters, swollen with sap and milk, churned memories of immortality with those of old poisons. Something of the Divine Consciousness still floated in the rivers.

Wars, dazzling, secretive, raged everywhere: amongst

men and monsters and insects. Insatiable desires surged within all beings, yet none dared set foot on the icy summit of the Himalayas, where Shiva reigned.

Huddled at the south-east corner of the Mountain was the minuscule kingdom of Mahisautha. Here, King Somdev gathered rumours from distant lands. Sal trees, glinting in the sun, surrounded the palace's flower-filled courtyard and put him in mind of Madhubani, the ancient city of Mithila, famed for its love of art and beauty.

"Will you too be called the 'Forest of Honey' some day?" he queried the blameless, unblemished trees. "I had a great number of your brethren chopped down to add columns to my palace, but to what avail? I no longer know where my duty lies, nor do I perceive the suffering of my people. I am desperate for a son."

Careful to tune his breathing to the wind's melody, Somdev was taking slow steps towards his favourite sal when strident voices caught his ear. Some servants, over by the kitchens:

"Am I a pig, a rooster, or a dog," grumbled one, "for the priests of Mahisautha to look upon me as impure?"

"Am I a woman afflicted with her menses or an impotent man," said another, "for them to treat me with such scorn?"

A third exclaimed that they were sure to be punished for raising their voices. By his lights, it seemed quite right that a foul being such as himself should eat from broken dishes and wear the clothes of the dead; and right it would remain, so long as the gods and history deemed it useful.

Somdev listened intently, holding his breath. He recognized the voice of the most deformed of his stable grooms: "The dwelling places of the Untouchables and the cooks are set apart, and we are barred from places of worship. For the most trivial violations, we are cursed to rot in hell. Such is our condition, but it will pass, as everything created by man passes. Let us focus rather on the ultimate reality because, outcaste or priest, our essence is equally divine."

At this, the others roared and pounced on the groom to hammer him. In the silence that followed, the king slumped against the trunk of his tree, sinking slowly to his knees. A moment later, he thought of taking counsel from Shiva's spouse—the goddess Durga, whom he worshipped above all others—but in the same instant there came up to him a stray dog, black-furred and purple-jowled, emerging unexpectedly from the deep shade of noon. Its eye sought an answering light in the king's, and it began licking his hands.

"Who are you?" mumbled Somdev, turning quite pale as fear pierced his heart. It was Shiva's dog, and bore on its back the god in his terrifying form... The king divined the three-eyed god: two of his eyes the sun and the moon to watch over Creation, and set between them the third eye, behind which lurked the fire that would destroy all existence if it went astray. The king tried to master himself, repeating that the third eye was not about to open. No, surely the end of the world wouldn't begin from this land, not in his time.

The dog loped away, disappearing down an unfamiliar path. Somdev thought he saw a woman carrying a rooster follow it, but they were swallowed up by the shadows. Soon, dust covered the surrounds of the palace, and then the entire kingdom. Puzzled, Somdev wrapped himself in a woollen blanket and hurried to his little temple. He would implore Durga to illumine his remaining days by sending him a son—even, perhaps, more than one.

2

Somdev was both wise and astute. He was in the habit of gathering around him men of letters, and discussing with them the life of the great Harshvardhana. He attempted to discern which of the mighty king's actions could mould his own destiny. An innate modesty prevented him from establishing foolish comparisons with the emperor: he was a minor raja and, unlike his role model, so he would remain. Harshvardhana had waged war often, to impose his rule over vast territories. The traveller Xuanzang came to sing his praises from as far away as China, such was the radiance of his insight and intelligence, suffused with poesy and the valour of a mighty warrior. But what survived of his immense power? Harshvardhana had not produced an heir. His wife having failed to birth a male, his empire lay in disarray.

Preparing unguents and powders before he could bow down to the goddess, Somdev looked through the peephole in the temple wall that allowed him to track the comings and goings of his subjects. His wife, Madoderi, was picking flowers in the garden. Somdev squinted, searching for the bed of precious marigolds that pleased Durga, and his brow grew furrowed: More beds would have to be planted right away, to keep the divinity's garlands refreshed.

The statue stood in its own dark recess at the back of the temple. The king grew emotional as he contemplated her inscrutable face and its glazed vermilion smile, her sparkling jewels. "Divine Durga, Great Mother, you well know that I lack a son, and it stands as an accusation against my character. What wrong have I done?"

On the implacable Durga's torso were the yellow, ruffle-skirted blossoms of marigold, concentrated points of light in the darkness. Somdev sensed that a message was imminent. As the goddess's vermilion lips opened a crack, her garlands began to tremble. They set themselves whirling in a giant wheel. "Heavens!" Somdev gasped in silence. "Does it fall to me to spin the wheel of mankind's fate? How came this symbol to be placed before my eyes?" The golden disc expanded, shrank, became copper, then iron. Dazzled at first by its splendour, the king began to grow deathly afraid, confused, unable to distinguish a thing. Wasn't the disc golden? Of gold, or at least good copper? Before he could finish his ablutions or apply the sindoor to his forehead, he fell like a log at the goddess's feet. Satisfied, she closed her lips, and the necklaces shrank again into two wilted garlands on her breast. Behind her perfectly modelled head with its sealed lips, a halo of tiny flames was yet aglow.

Laid out on silk cushions when Somdev came to, his eyes opened on a purple-hued firmament fading to pure white, and he thought for a moment he had achieved everlasting bliss. But the palace servants rushing over, fans in hand, dispelled the impression, as did the crowd of worried dignitaries not daring to draw near. He could easily guess what was being whispered: weakness in a king harms the cosmic order. "The cosmos has nothing to fear," he thought to himself. "I have always performed the ritual sacrifices as per the rules." Alas, the greatest disaster that could befall a glorious lineage, or for that matter an unremarkable one, was the lack of a male descendant. Somdev judged his own lineage was of the second order, even if he was a descendant of the Sun.

He let the servants fuss over him before sitting up on the silk cushions, his back ramrod straight, legs tucked under him so that his strength, gathered in, wouldn't leak out wastefully. Eyes half-closed he took a deep breath, waiting for a divine sign that would save the kingdom of Mahisautha. Madoderi appeared, his graceful spouse, having finished her flower-picking. She was running towards him, a blur in a long, mauve veil. He saw Durga's tiger escorting her. Garbed in purple and gold, his wife's form rippled and her face was white as milk. The tiger girded her waist with its tail, a twisted belt of fire. The transfigured rani next appeared flanked by an immaculate elephant and horse. A golden orb burst from the summit of the Himalayas, like the top blown off a volcano. Abandoning the heavenly sphere, it sped towards the palace, swerving to the queen's luminous silhouette. Somdev thought he might faint again. Was he really meant to witness such prodigies? The vision wavered between a huge ball and a light-emanating wheel spinning at unthinkable speed. In the blink of an eye, the magical circle had shrunk to the size of a chickpea and disappeared. Somdev barely had time to see his wife's mouth open and her arms wave in the air, or notice one of her bare feet strike the ground, before a bountiful tree sprang up at the very spot, and he knew she was pregnant through divine intercession.

▼

Mahisautha wasn't exactly in the shadow of the Himalayas, at a distance in fact. But the Mountain rose so prodigiously that up to the farthest end of the Earth the soil remained Shiva's and none could prove otherwise. The Lord's matchless generosity was such, and such the power of the couple he formed with Durga, that he could have blown every kingdom off the earth in a sneeze, flattening humans and non-humans, sending them back to their shared essence.

Durga watched closely over the queen's pregnancy, as a priest is careful with the ladleful of ghee he is about to tip into his cauldron. A girl named Bansapti, or 'Goddess of the Forest', was born, and the court arranged its features to a welcome of polite disappointment. "May it please Shiva for my wife to bear more children," thought Somdev. "Observing the rites fastidiously will ensure that I get a son one day."

His faith impressed the gods residing on the Mountain. Once Somdev came to feel a vast, stable love towards all beings in the universe, including his neighbours—human and others, whether they swung from the trees, crawled in the dust, or sped through air or water—the divine couple saw that he was mature enough to welcome a son who would outdo him in goodness, wisdom and valour. The son would grow up to be a finer man than Harshvardhana the Warrior, because his nobility would be that of Love.

Durga protected the vessel of the queen, who gave birth first to one son, and then two more. After which, the excellent frame being worn out, the rani died. She had brought forth four magnificent trees: Bansapti, Jaybhardan, Moti Ram and Budeshwar. Moti Ram meant 'Rama's Pearl', while Budeshwar was seen as the 'Joyful Tree'. Jaybhardan, the eldest son, was in the eyes of all who saw him 'The Greatest of Trees'. Known by the name of Salhesh, 'King of the Mountain', his fame would extend to the farthest reaches of the inhabited Earth.

3

On the night that followed the birth of Jaybhardan, another male child blessed by the Invisibles arrived in the wash of the powerful goddess Ganga. Now all sweetness, now crazed arrogance, Ganga let herself be adored under the eye of the Master of the Himalayas, he whose three dread eyebrows were quick to furrow. Their story ran yet in the valleys and the plains, where Shiva's devotees knotted their hair in tribute to the time their Lord had saved the Earth from total devastation. When Ganga first took the form of a river and burst from the Mountain's body, Shiva had thrown himself beneath it to break her fall with his matted locks. Ever since, those of keen hearing could detect the roar of Ganga's waters in the growls of Durga's tiger.

The male child was born in Mokama, a little south of Mithila. His mother was a sister to Somdev, one he hadn't seen in years and who had indeed been forgotten. This child's existence began like all others: the proper birth rites were performed over the labouring woman—hair undone, garbed in her ugliest sari, as was customary. A midwife arrived, to massage the mother and child on a bed of twigs sheltered behind a closed door, to prepare medicinal plants and unguents, and to anticipate every need, whether in the immediate present or for eternity. Which didn't keep her from being regarded as lower than the sole of a foot.

That night, the sun and the moon, together with a fabulous tree that bloomed at twilight, the harsingar, conspired that darkness should not cover the sky. At the newborn boy's first wail, thousands of harsingar jasmines bloomed from Mahisautha to Mokama, without concern for time or season. Women who arose early in the morning were surprised to see myriad little white helices strewing the ground, each dotted with the bright orange of saffron offerings. Some women pointed out that the hue was gaudier than usual, like blood even, but they refrained from warning the new mother in her confinement hut, and she never learned of the strange day that had dawned.

Following custom, female friends and relatives were invited to the ceremony set to take place in a hastily built cabin a few days after the birth. Only now, relieved of her dirty, ragged clothes, bathed, coiffed, perfumed and dressed in yellow, could the new mother be approached by visitors, all offering advice as they awaited the most critical moment of the ceremony: presenting the infant to 'He who decides the child's fate'. That would take place before the eastern wall. The mother smiled wanly at a skeletal ancestor as wrinkled as the Thar, and the old woman showed everyone a clay doll she had made herself—the Scribe of Fate. She took her time, the better to impress those in attendance, before abruptly stabbing the clay with a bamboo stem fitted with a flat, dry leaf. All that remained was for the fissured clay statuette to trace the pattern of fateful signs. The audience shuddered, and the mother closed her eyes.

When she opened them, she was in the next world, or the misty corridor leading there, because the cabin had caught fire, and all within, except for the newborn, had perished.

On the banks of the river glimmering with memories of the Great Battle of the Kauravas and the Pandavas, village women gathered bulrushes to make a cradle for the infant. The women could never have dreamt that two male children—the son and nephew of Somdev, King of Mahisautha—had just been born to oppose each other.

Later, people would claim that a stray dog had snatched the newborn from the burning house and brought him to a wet nurse. The good woman took the child in and completed the rituals. She soothed the foundling, unknotted his nerves with mustard oil, stimulated his body with an enveloping massage, and eliminated any evil spirits lurking perchance in the folds of his flesh. Then she brought him to a high-ranking family in Mokama.

▼

The boy born at the river's edge, of good bones and muscles, was given the name Chuharmal. The two cousins' early years passed without mishap. Unaware of each other, both were equally keen, after being trained in virile behaviour, to dash at full tilt into life. In honourable families, a boy's education was based on the idea that each man expressed a particular aspect of the infinite divinity. He was to move towards the Divine Source, step by step, by demonstrating his qualities. With their intelligence and their senses fully awake, Jaybhardan and Chuharmal applied themselves to honing their faculties and their subtle bodies until the small-minded, fearful, selfish and blind self melted into the cosmos. Indifferent to the frivolous activities that appealed to their friends, they learned to restrain their emotions.

This early in life, no one could have suspected the great rivalry to come at the foot of the Mountain—no one but the Scribe of Fate, whose doll of clay had been wrecked and dispersed. For the moment, both boys aspired to rid themselves of vanity, certain that they would never wish to range themselves against their fellow men; they believed their gratitude to the universe would express itself in loving kindness towards its component beings, all fruits of the same Divine Consciousness.

4

To the leader of his troops Somdev entrusted his own three sons and Karikant, his daughter's son, to be trained as their rank required. First, however, came the morning rituals, performed before the two sacred trees that stood outside the palace: "The sun rises at the peak of the oblation," as the saying went. The Brahmin who served the royal court carried out his task under the watchful eyes of the teenagers lined up near their father and grandfather. Next, the youngsters fell into step behind the rugged man whose task it was to turn them into supreme athletes, into fighters capable of slicing other young men to pieces. The king, who was repulsed by violence, found no thrill in the idea of war. To forestall the possibility, he made sure to impress on the people of Mahisautha, and more importantly those of neighbouring lands, his eternal readiness for war. He had strengthened the cavalry and multiplied the number of his elephants by seven, to reach a total of forty-nine: the number of magical phonemes in the sacred alphabet. It wasn't for nothing that another of Somdev's names was 'Shiva's assistant'.

The organization of his earthly affairs offered but a glimpse of his disposition to square with divinity, in fact Somdev grabbed at every chance to include the Lord in his projects. Derisory as they may be, he still nursed a quiet hope of gaining his Lord's support. Durga's help in conceiving his progeny had reinforced his optimism: the day would come when Jaybhardan the Great Tree would ride the fiftieth elephant.

The fiftieth phoneme had a wondrous, secret character, whose meaning escaped ordinary mortals. Somdev himself had not yet grasped it fully. He did entertain the possibility of this accomplishment, supreme on Earth as in Heaven; a hope he dared mention only to his guru—who had been living like a hermit deep inside a cave in the Himalayas for so long he was assumed to be immortal. Somdev had delayed and hesitated over requesting the guru's assistance in completing Jaybhardan's education. His eldest son needed to develop a steely mind that both gods and men could rely on. Should the master agree to take Jaybhardan's education in hand, he may as well take on the other three—Moti Ram, Budeshwar and Karikant—so that one day they might form a first-rate phalanx around the heir to the throne.

No one knew how the king reached the holy man in his hiding place, but the four youngsters believed he had ridden there on the back of the elephant-headed god. Ganesha had transmitted the Vedas to the world. He wore the fifty signs corresponding to the sacred phonemes in a necklace. He must have flapped his ears to fly up to the grotto, like a giant butterfly. The boys were sure of it.

▼

Somdev set out to see the guru convinced the somewhat eccentric old man wouldn't refuse him, especially in a task that would find favour with Shiva.

Paying no mind to the shrieks of hyenas prowling in the sylvan dark, he slipped into the hermit's cave where he found the guru waiting, twinkly-eyed, for him.

"Finally," said the wizened man, "you didn't show much haste."

The guru's creased, weather-worn body looked like an old cloth soaked in water and slapped against a washing stone.

"You certainly took your time," he continued with pursed lips, "before coming to me about your boys. Do you think I didn't know what was going on down there?"

The king bowed low and apologized profusely.

"Don't start that, for goodness' sake," the wizened mouth replied. "Relax, Somdev. Take some betel with me, and let's get started. Would you like some tobacco with your areca nut?"

A wrinkled hand darted out from his shrivelled mess of flesh, flying up to pull two large wilted leaves out of a pouch. How many hands did the guru have hidden amid all those folds? Four? Eight? Crouched on legs twisted into a knot, he looked like a cobra. His torso seemed to sway in readiness, as though vibrating, and mossy hair crowned him like a white hood.

"Good fate requires meticulous preparation, master," the king murmured. "My sons are not yet ready to marry; I want to perfect their education first."

"Excellent," the guru replied. "All the better since the eldest will never take a wife."

Somdev felt faint with dread. No woman? It was inconceivable!

In one move the wise man folded all his hands over his belly. Calm arrived, settling in a slow swirl; then he opened his mouth. On his tongue, the betel nut had made a small puddle of blood. His body was perfectly motionless as he spoke in a deadpan voice: "I see before me the leader of your troops with his soldiers lined up in rows. He is teaching them to run like antelopes and to slither along like serpents. He teaches them to disguise themselves as lions or trees for camouflage, but he teaches them neither the inner strength of trees, nor their sensitivity, nor even the intelligence of cobras."

Somdev sat chewing on his lips. This was exactly—word for word—what had passed through his mind on the way here.

"He allows them to gain something in the way of endurance, and the experience of struggle. There is synchronization, which certainly counts," allowed the scrawny old man. "But are they going to practise with a long stick until they're grown men?"

Somdev gritted his teeth. The guru went on, permitting his gaze to drift, "The long stick is fine for keeping the wrists supple, but a little girl could overcome it... Now they're in a defensive stance, holding this bit of wood over their heads, their eyes gone white, pupils drawn under the lids to frighten their adversaries."

Confused, Somdev lowered his eyes. The guru laboured the point, "Tell me, Somdev, when do they move on to the curved stick?"

He must mean the thing vaguely reminiscent of an elephant tusk, but weren't they used more in the south—somewhat akin to the art of imitating animals. So far as Somdev knew, the guru had never lived in the south.

"So you know everything, master?" the king muttered.

The old man chortled, a string of red spittle dribbling down his chin. "Rest assured," he said, clasping the king's hands affectionately. "I know what your boys need. The worthy soldier who trains them is teaching them to conquer with strength. Don't rebuke him, but entrust your sons to my care. I will reveal to them the lessons of our Divine Mother."

The king nodded contentedly, but the old man wasn't done. "Nature. Her action can destabilize the intelligence of men who think they have a monopoly on reason."

The king nodded again. "Yes, I see."

"Do you know why caterpillars nibble around the edges of leaves, Somdev? Tell me, why don't they chomp at the very heart of the leaf they mean to devour? They never even touch it."

"Because the outer edges are more tender?" the king hazarded.

The guru folded his arms back into his thousand folds, disappearing almost completely, sucked into his own centre. The wind in the cedars that protected his hiding place held its breath. Finally, with a vague stroking movement, the old man unfolded himself once again.

"Perhaps nature sees further than immediate predation," he suggested.

"Or perhaps what is essential is some learning, to take into account the full range of equilibriums that need to be maintained on earth. Take, absorb, reject: that hasty cycle satisfies ordinary men. They focus on the outcome of their actions, which flatters their personal pride. Your sons and grandson will be different. Karikant, Moti Ram and Budeshwar will serve Jaybhardan. He will be Salhesh, the King of the Himalayas."

Silence descended, charged with awe. Disconcerted, in a hurry to be gone, Somdev bowed low to the ground, brushing the old man's feet with his fingertips. One who aspires to tread in the field of felicity must guard against being overwhelmed, he reminded himself, chewing on his betel. On the way back to the palace, he would apply himself, as so often before, to mastering his fears and desires.

Somdev was at the mouth of the cave when the old man sprang towards him in a single bound. As a flaming eye opened in the middle of his forehead, the scarlet slot of his mouth spat out the words, "Salhesh will face three trials, do you hear me, Somdev, my friend?"

He jabbed three fingers towards the king. The king saw three times three, then, suddenly, forty-nine. The old man turned as black as an embalmed corpse and repeated, "Three trials: seductive women, magical temptations... and himself, naturally!"

With that, the old man waggled his tongue at him,

roared with laughter loud enough to rock the Mountain, and vanished into his cave.

5

Time went by, the sun continued to rise without fail, sparkling on Shiva's trishul, the trident named 'Victory', that the Brahmin polished at dawn. Built on the spot where Jaybhardan was born, the temple with its carved front displayed the god himself, flanked by a white bull, grasping his trishul firmly, a crescent moon in his hair: all the attributes in place. Greeting him each morning, dignitaries and servants alike were reminded of the true nature of the world.

"Essence, energy, passivity... the decisive qualities of primordial nature," the Brahmin recited as he rubbed the trishul, steeping its metal in the attributes he was invoking. "The pure and good essence of things: the luminous principle. Energy... watch out for ambivalence! Beware of passions and feelings that disturb energy! Passivity: misery of miseries, obscurity makes its nest in inertia."

"Essence, luminosity and goodness..." echoed the neighbouring sal trees.

"What is perishable issues from the imperishable and returns to it," whispered the birds. "Why brood over what is certain to pass?"

▼

As the guru launched the teenagers' education in the forest, their cousin Chuharmal was by the river Ganga, training to become a wrestler. His teacher was Bhima the Terrible, named after one of the heroes of the Great Battle, who, legend has it, split an elephant in half with the side of his hand.

The details of the story had been obscured by time, but the exact spot where the story unfolded was well known: the Great Battle had taken place not too far from where Chuharmal was training.

The wrestling pit, dug into the ground, was four cubits deep and topped with a dome of bamboo poles rising four cubits, yielding a cube-shaped arena. Bhima compared the structure to a temple's vimana: "The tower, the backbone of the sanctuary. Think of the centre of the arena as the divinity's navel, my son."

To ensure the quality of both physical and spiritual education, the wrestler trained just four teenagers at a time. Chuharmal, with the character and makings of a leader, was a role model to the other three. The others—Mohendra, Birendra and Karakulak the Jackal, peasants' sons all—worshipped him to an extent that was almost damaging, because it made him harder to control. As for teaching Chuharmal to control his own feelings, it was no easy task.

Every day, Bhima would go down into the arena, salute Mother Earth and invite his pupils to follow his example. He would say, "Your turn, sons of the Earth," and they would all enter the clay pit right foot first, as was the custom, after sweeping one leg around in a circle to inform the space that they claimed it in every dimension. The space was inhabited by powers that could not be driven out, but whom they could try to pacify with the right show of force. The sons of the earth would march forward, their eyes boring into the western wall towards the shrine of Hanuman, the god with the face of a monkey. Small flames and flowers were arranged in an alternating pattern on the rack ascending from the altar. Their weapons, each on its dedicated altar, received the same offerings of flowers and fire. The mantras rising between the red-clay walls completed the process of turning the arena into a magical structure.

The boys moved forward in silence, with both pride and humility: drawing themselves up to their full height, they walked with supple steps to keep their physiological and mental capacities in balance. Each knew which primordial elements connected him to his energies—the earth and water from which the clay had been kneaded; fire, air and ether—and each boy performed the rituals with mindfulness.

Bhima's knowledge was unsophisticated but accurate. He knew that an unhealthy body not only kept a wrestler from winning his bout, it also prevented the mind from elevating itself, by obliging it to focus on more material concerns. Performing their physical exercises correctly depended on cultivating a simultaneous, worshipful frame of mind. When Chuharmal, Mohendra, Birendra and Karakulak the Jackal had bowed before the serpent who symbolically guarded the arena, touched the ground first with their right hands then their foreheads, and finally, prostrated themselves before Hanuman's shrine, the divinity would purify their blood and hearts, and Mother Earth would be satisfied.

Meanwhile, Somdev's sons were given over to meditation, faces turned to their guru. Seated in the lotus position, left foot on right thigh and right foot on left, they formed perfect triangles. Any fatuous talk was out of the question, but neither could they simply keep quiet. "Being in silence" was what was required of them. Where studying and sexual abstinence were necessary forms of austerity, silence was not. A prerequisite for expanding the consciousness, it offered itself as an infinite luxuriance. The adept had to find the key to the treasure within himself, where the two vital currents, the centripetal and the centrifugal, merged, engendering a middle state that opened on to subtler levels. It may have been difficult to understand, but the guru's attitude brooked no debate. The phases of a well-guided mystical life would gradually be revealed to them, and Jaybhardan, Moti Ram, Budeshwar and Karikant would have no time to go astray. Discipline would always pull them back into its analogous cycles, those of the universe.

"Everything is in everything," the old man reminded them with succinct confidence. "Each cycle contains what the others will develop. Do not yield to the temptation of dazzling speed! What dazzles too quickly soon fades away."

His disciples remained impassive.

"Stable, peaceful reality will be revealed to you

when the perception in your bodies has changed," the guru continued with burning eyes. His ascendancy over Somdev came from the fact that he had received one day a vision of the syllable 'Om'. 'Seeing' the primordial sound vibration was a rare privilege, and one that had made the old man inflexible. Other boys might have harboured doubts about the cosmic marvels he dangled before them, but not Jaybhardan. Nor Moti Ram, Budeshwar or Karikant. They knew that the infinite would spill from the old man's ragged lips. Sitting beneath the trees, they waited for the sacred syllable to rise from that misshapen body, and the guru peered deep into their dark eyes to learn what was stirring within. Were they still restive, or had they grown settled? To prepare them for an uninterrupted spiritual witness, he urged that from the splendid forest where they sat, they picture vast, bare spaces. The exercise made the mind more pliable by training it to become detached from visual stimulation. Considerations of beauty and its terms could come later.

On their return to the palace, the boys continued training with the cavalrymen, or, in the case of the eldest, his apprenticeship in taming elephants. Living in harmony with those huge creatures offered nothing but advantages. The head mahout loved elephants, creatures related to mankind because both had been fashioned by the gods from the same clay. Besides, the elephant's trunk had earned it the nickname, 'He who has an arm in the middle of his face'.

"Between men and elephants," the mahout, who sometimes ran out of arguments, insisted, "the connection isn't based on physical resemblance, as with monkeys. It is more internal."

Soon the king wanted his son to have his own elephant—the fiftieth elephant, a harbinger of unprecedented marvels.

The mahout presented him a hulking specimen with a good, reliable gaze, who would grow and age with him. His name was Bhuranand. The king congratulated the mahout on his excellent choice and entrusted Jaybhardan with the responsibility of a square garden in the middle of which he could house the elephant. Later, he would hand over the entire royal estate, with its hundreds of admirable beasts, to Jaybhardan's custody. Somdev was pushing himself to do things on a scale to satisfy celestial intentions, so a gratified fate might favour the leadership of an enlightened son over Mahisautha.

▼

At a ceremony attended only by important dignitaries, Jaybhardan received a small trishul made especially for him, to use as a hook. The elephant keeper always carried one as an indispensable symbol of authority between the two powers: man and elephant. In theory, the mahout never needed to use the trishul. If on a whim he decided to hang it on his ride's ear in a moment of trust, it was still his prerogative to grab for it and assert the upper hand. Their shared history forced him to do so: men had assaulted these peaceable giants in order to domesticate them... with only relative success, on account of the seed of freedom the divinity had planted in both elephants and men. The mahout had always to dominate the beast, even in the best collaboration, even where the strongest affection sprang up. The head mahout had spoken to the prince at great length about the pachyderms who shaded the outer edges of the eastern territories in grey. At the first hint of danger, the herd would dash, single file, deep into the jungle at the foot of the Mountain, their minds tormented by memories of human cruelty, their brothers' capture, atrocious amputations.

"Human intelligence is slacker than that of elephants," the mahout said ruefully. "Serving it can only be detrimental to the quality of their soul."

Seeing Jaybhardan seated so majestically on Bhuranand moved Somdev profoundly in his gradual advance towards death. Painful ideas would sometimes surge over and over in his mind, but he was consoled by the thought that transferring the emblems of royalty to his son would soon allow him to retire to a quiet little hermitage in the forest. He focused on the image of Jaybhardan as a brilliant representative of the very tradition he himself had served so faithfully. He would soon be disabused of this notion.

Mounted astride Bhuranand, when the prince grasped the trishul, his legs prolonged by those of the extraordinary beast were as the limb pillars of a living temple, of which he was the fragile vimana, the steeple connecting heaven and earth. Although he jabbed with the prod like an impatient novice, his father glimpsed in a flash the seamless, elemental being his son would become: a pioneer of love who would blaze an original and unpredictable path through the world.

7

The cousins, Jaybhardan and Chuharmal, reached the age of eighteen without ever having met. They came into manhood with much the same responsibilities, their separate lives punctuated by rites of passage, of initiation and accession. In Somdev's court, Shiva and his intimates, Durga and Ganesha, were worshipped with the greatest ardency. Around Bhima, it was Hanuman, patron of wrestlers, able to lift mountains and leap over the Himalayas, who drew fervid devotion. Each year's festival was an occasion for the athletes to smarten the deity's statue with a fresh coat of paint, or better yet, offer the god a new statue to inhabit. The increment of an arm or extra head was always possible, Hanuman being not only extensible but a divinity of parts, doctor and grammarian. A marked preference for one deity didn't rule out prudence towards the others, and everyone, whether in Mokama or Mahisautha, was preparing to honour Hanuman at the coming full moon. Besides, nowhere was it implied that any god was more important than another within the Divine Oneness.

Gurus knew that diversity troubled their disciples. It demoralized a conquering mind out to establish hierarchies and separations within the phenomenal jungle. The wisest course lay in recognizing an essential, palpable, ever-changing communion, and to admit that it eluded classification; but the quest for an ideal order poisoned the world. Gurus were sometimes delighted to see the bafflement of their most perfectionist pupils: there was something to be said for the pandemonium of existence if it could stymie the rebellious and the prideful—who were often one and the same. The gods had set a neat trap. Probabilities that looked incompatible at first came to be linked together by slow degrees, till the seeker's prior conditioning gave way under the strain and its exhausted remnants turned to flotsam, trailing in the wake of life's ceaseless meandering. Disciples had to learn to forswear the attractions of definite knowledge, the better to cope with the likelihood that real life would turn out less simple. For the mind this was the price of grace, in its approach to Divine Oneness. The mind's liberation required first submitting to a humble rest, renouncing the wish to dominate everything in sight.

▼

Bhima hadn't thought any of this through in detail. He was sure of just one thing: in order to survive, you had to know how to act in several different ways or on several different levels at once. In his teaching, he intertwined the subtle and the concrete, and summarized the lesson succinctly in three phases: reach, release, place at rest. Reach, release. Place at rest. Subtlety could only be cultivated at rest: this proved a stumbling block for Chuharmal. Bhima had trained some seven hundred athletes over a lifetime, and not one measured up to

Chuharmal, not even his three unflinching companions, Mohendra, Birendra and Karakulak the Jackal. The four of them, Bhima liked to say, were like "the fingers of a hand whose thumb was Hanuman". But Chuharmal's pride did need to be taken down a peg. Blind passion roiled beneath it, hot-headedness to the point of violence when someone refused to submit to him. Such pride revealed an ungodly lack of realism, which did not bode well. Chuharmal's weakness was the supreme confidence he placed in his own self, rather than entrusting himself to nature, of which he was but one tiny product.

So far, Bhima had spared him the pain of humiliation in front of his peers. The time had now come for Bhima to seek Hanuman's guidance and rectify the fault for good.

Hanuman appeared to him in the twilight, jewelled from knuckles to biceps, his chest slashed open. He spread the gash with his own hands to bring forth Rama and Sita, the lovers revered throughout the Ganga plain. Bhima bowed before the statue, and nothing happened. Unwontedly, his gaze fell on the gentle goddess Sita, and at once he knew how to bring a useful lesson home to his Chuharmal, who was drunk on the absolute. Rama was the champion of immutable order, but Sita introduced something more flexible, a happy medium that excluded the absolute and didn't enclose facts in dogma.

▼

Convinced that his stiff-necked pupil required a feminine corrective, if not to humble him then at least to introduce a little balance, Bhima bowed again quickly and climbed out of the wrestlers' pit, looking cheerful. He invited the young men to a drink of lassi down by the river.

"The statue is crumbling," he announced. "Its paint is flaking and bits of the statue keep coming off with it."

Mohendra and Birendra were gnawing at the twigs they had used to stir their lassi.

"That's a job for women, isn't it?" Karakulak the Jackal objected. "Can't our aunts and girl cousins from Madhubani deal with it? I hear they have even been invited to Mokama to touch up the designs on the temples along the riverbank."

Birendra joined the discussion. "It's the tradition in Mithila; these women are born with a bamboo paintbrush in their hands. In no time, they'll have Hanuman good as new for you."

"No, I expect you to handle it," Bhima snapped back. "No one else shall touch Hanuman."

He fixed a meaningful look at Chuharmal, who remained silent.

"The honour is yours. Go down into the arena, bow to Hanuman and examine his condition carefully. The paint on his knees and around the eyes is chipping away, but I want you to clean the whole statue first and repaint it, right up to applying the finish with the black outlines and the pupils."

Picturing Chuharmal at this dainty task, Mohendra

bent double with laughter. Chuharmal raised his chin incredulously.

"The pupil is faded," Bhima stated in a voice that brooked no objection. "The eye has lost its lustre."

Pleased to poke fun at his friend, Mohendra added, "There's a row of rubies in the middle of the crown that also wants a spot of touching up."

Chuharmal ignored him, kept his chin resolute and his gaze fixed on the distance.

"You are the best of us, Chuharmal," Bhima cut in, in a changed tone of voice. "Therefore, be careful, my son. The death you glimpse in the pupil of another is your own, make sure you get that into your head."

"... And the cosmic order is maintained by sacrifice," the young man finished the thought silently. It was an oft-repeated lesson. His descent from the moon flashed in his mind. The figure of death was connected to the radiant sun and said to be born of an impious, excessive presumption. What had made him think of it now?

"Tonight," Bhima added quickly. His voice grew dull, muffled, arriving like an echo from the distance. "Afterwards, retire to the hillside and invoke the Son of the Wind. Meditate on your vocation as a warrior, focusing on his achievements, his unblemished righteousness and his loyalty towards Rama. Towards Sita, too."

Chuharmal went tense and his skin darkened.

Was night falling already? Soon his outline would be hard to distinguish in the obscurity.

"Go, Chuharmal," breathed Bhima softly, tired now.

"My teaching is at an end. Go and receive Hanuman's."

His voice faded. And a mist settled between them.

"What I did not know how to inculcate in you, he will be able to. Today you lead three valiant companions. Some day, they will be legion."

His words died as if they had travelled over a distance. All of a sudden, his face wilted. He let his head droop to the chest, brought his hands together and gestured ever so lightly towards the entrance of the arena. The shadows had nearly consumed them. Mohendra, Birendra and Karakulak the Jackal brought their hands together in turn, and bowed to touch their leader's feet. Moonlight spilled over Chuharmal, revealing his savage beauty. It accentuated each muscle of his chest, shoulders and face, illumined the broad arc of his avid mouth, hung its light on the too-plump lip and disappeared behind the wing of a bird of prey. Before the watchful eyes of his stunned companions, he went wordlessly down into the red-clay pit as darkness settled again over the arena.

▼

It was a tense night in the celestial abode. The roots of his heart grew inverted, like the sacrificial fig tree, and he could feel, almost tangibly, that time was withering the world. The pit began to gush with lava. He slipped and fell to the incandescent ground. "Here is my fear," he thought, "its eyes gaping distraught at furious shapes. I see my fear. Woe unto me! Which god now turns the

Cosmic Wheel? Who swings my blood between two existences?"

"Have mercy," he wailed, unnerved by violent shoves in the dark, "I am too young to renounce the fruits of the body. Am I dead? Do I live yet?"

The tumult ceased abruptly, and waves of pure water streamed over his face, while a gentle persuasion penetrated his bones. His fears and desires fell away one by one; exhausted, he dreamt of a lapse into innocence. But just when he thought he had been saved, the statue suddenly moved. The little oil lamps arranged on the rack blazed all at once, as Hanuman drew himself up—a giant with arms like the boles of cedars, thighs as ropy and powerful as baobab trunks. The god's body was wood, stone and sand; he was air and water and infinite space, solidity and rarefaction, immutable essence. Hanuman stepped out of his statue and strode towards Chuharmal. Seized with dumb fury, the athlete's head began to shake: the Indus, Ganga, and Brahmaputra sprayed from his skull, flowing down his face and the sides of his chest in torrents braided with his own sweat. He leapt up, and with a roar, grabbed hold of the divine body with all his strength. Jewels glittered against his knuckles and biceps. Instantly, a ball of fire rolled over him, and making a hundred thousand mirrors on his skin, it burst into flames. When he was entirely alight, the crystal of the mountain appeared to him in all its facets. He collapsed to the ground, and the pit began to fill with ashes over him.

The nearby sal trees whispered to the banyans that the combat had lasted an aeon, but the demons and titans who swirled in limbo swore it was over in the blink of an eye.

Chuharmal finally opened his eyes. He raised himself shakily, brushing off the bits of clay stuck to his body, and saw Hanuman's shattered statue at the foot of the shrine in front of the western wall. The floor of the pit held shards of the broken image strewn amidst smoking oil lamps. He knelt in prayer before them and stepped out of the arena lacerated by the shadows of noon. The sun blazed at its zenith. Remembering what Bhima had said, he headed slowly towards the hill, like a poor man who aspires only for the ultimate silence.

8

Across the lands of the ancient kingdom of Mithila, women prepared for the festival of Hanuman by painting his achievements on the walls of their homes. Several communities huddled in the creased folds at the foot of the Mountain, especially the Dusadh from Madhubani and the Malin from the land of Morang—who prided themselves on their knowledge of the marshlands' medicinal flowers and plants. The Malins had penetrated the mysteries of the Earth. It was said that the women were magicians with bizarre rites, similar to the creatures who danced while seated, their arms undulating to overwhelm men's senses. It was also said that they could sometimes be glimpsed locked in an embrace with nagas, the venomous serpents that infested the countryside. Among them were three wondrously beautiful sisters who had been sent to the neighbouring kingdoms for their skill in painting floral motifs: Dauna, Kushuma and Reshma—the youngest and most impetuous of the three.

Somdev had relatives among the Dusadh. He was planning to honour the heroes of the *Ramayana* and wanted to dedicate a room in his palace to Rama and Sita, Hanuman's protégés, in order to prepare his sons for the idea of getting married. For the moment they seemed uninterested, Jaybhardan still less inclined than the others, but the king refused to take the guru's prediction about his first-born son to heart. For advice he turned to the women who had exclusive rights on drawing the heroes and heroines of the saga. They had recommended Dauna and Kushuma for the floral borders on the walls and pillars. And if they were coming here, Somdev thought he might as well get them to freshen the paint on Shiva's ornaments beneath the trees.

A king named Bhim Sain reigned from the palace of Pakaria, south of Morang. The palace was surrounded by a marvellous garden, where the king's daughter, Princess Chandravati, lived. Like any paradise, the princess's garden was surrounded by walls, but she had complained of them to her father. If the walls must stand, couldn't he at least have them painted over and made less obvious? Of course he could. Bhim Sain sent a messenger north, to find him a young woman capable of expressing the magnificence of nature; Reshma was recommended.

The gods ordered her to go first to Mokama, by the river Ganga, then to Pakaria. No one listened to her protests that Mokama was terribly out of the way and would make for a long detour.

Because the three sisters were magicians, and only young girls, neither the head of their community, nor even their own parents worried about their journeying over such distances. The parents settled for entrusting them to Hanuman's protection. The Son of the Wind would turn all feline and hyena snouts away. He would escort them to Mahisautha, Mokama and Pakaria.

Their parents gave them a few sprigs of a plant called durva, which the Brahmins used during their rituals;

it was known for quelling the demon of eclipses. Then they waved and let them go. Being parents, a stubborn part of them was certain their girls would encounter an ancient green-skinned monster, Durvasas, along the way and would never be seen again.

The first stage of Reshma's journey was peaceful. She was troubled neither by the heat nor the cold. The deer welcomed her each night into the warmth of their flanks, and she could tell that the sal trees were hard at work inside their barks, renewing their leaves, dreaming of luminous inflorescences and fluttering seeds. After hours of walking, Reshma dozed off against a sal trunk, her eyes drooping but her nose alert to the scents around her. Shimmering beings grazed her cheeks, the Invisibles rocked her in their arms. She pondered how Ganga allowed souls to unite with their ultimate truths, and wondered what the palace of Pakaria and Princess Chandravati's garden would be like. She dreamt of paradise.

The city of Mokama rose on the other side of the river, as if from its bed. On the bank, birds gathered over her. She recognized the little green parrots that are said to be evil omens, and noticed that the bees that had been following her since she'd left home had disappeared. The edges of the Ganga seemed shrivelled. She looked for a footbridge or a place to ford the river, for the riverbed struck her as dark and slimy. In preparation for the crossing, she raised a protective stockade around her heart and gobbled down what was left of her provisions for the journey. That was when fear swooped in and her soul began to darken. A group of local villagers was getting ready to cross the river on elephant-back. Abandoning all modesty, Reshma whipped off her veil and waved it in their direction, shouting at the top of her lungs. The men looked at her warily, but one of the elephants ambled over to sniff her with its trunk. She embraced it with childlike joy, and the animal hoisted her carefully on to its back alongside the bags of mangoes already there. The mahout assented churlishly.

"Thank Ganga, fallen woman," he snapped at Reshma, with a hard look.

The girl's toes grazed the water, her veil floating behind like a train. Once back on solid ground, she thanked both elephant and mahout before sitting down in the shade of a fig tree to watch the little procession move on. Once the figures had faded in the distance, she felt someone's eyes on her: a muscular older man with gleaming lips who hadn't left with the others. She swiftly jerked the veil back over her face, and the cloth wrapped itself around her in a tight protective sheath.

"Don't you come near me!" she shrieked. The man's lips curled up, showing rotten teeth.

"Divine Mother," Reshma prayed silently, "will you save me?" But the man loomed over her now, and fear gripped her heart. Not a single mantra came to her. She probed the depths of her being, frantic to summon some counteractive energy, but in her kidneys and her liver she found nothing but fear lashing soundlessly. She grabbed at it, soaking it into her secret humours and every last drop of blood, almost savouring it. The man raised a hand towards her. Dread laughter twitched on her lips. Then Reshma gathered her strength and let rip with a long, piercing wail. A cobra rose from the ground, barely three inches from the man. Startled, he stepped back and scurried away in fear.

The serpent slid away into the rocks, and Reshma, her body empty, sank to her knees and burst into tears.

"Alas," she sighed, "who will save me from the turbulence called man?"

But she couldn't help smiling when she thought of the sea monster that was the goddess Ganga's mount. Jaws of a crocodile, tail of a fish, and trunk of an elephant. A chimeric animal, it was her own makara, and it had allowed her to cross the river. She gave thanks for her deliverance.

As night fell, she caught sight of a flare burning on a hilltop, and let herself be guided by it. The glow had such a pull she ran all the way up. Was she climbing the celestial Mount Meru? The elders said it was encircled by smaller mountains... Had she crossed the range unawares? Her feet flew over stones to reach the marvellous holy mount: its white face turned to the east, red to the north, brown—or was it black?—to the west... And the south face? Yellow. The southern face was yellow. Now she was running with all her strength, panting and out of breath. But where were the seven concentric rings the wise men spoke of... and what about the seven climates and seven seas? Still running, she counted on her fingers: the salty sea and the enchanted sea, the sea of sugar and the sea of butter, the sea of milk and curd, the sea of nectar and the freshwater sea... She kept running, running... But what if she were wrong? Must the greatest joy always be stippled with doubt? A surge of anger rose in her throat. Was she to be smeared with dread yet again?

High above her, the fire glowed. Reshma's eyes filled with tears. Breathless, she wiped them quickly. Now she was shown a giant lotus—with its leaves and its seeds. A store of gemstones piled in a huge vase. What was the meaning of this ascent? Her body was propelling itself to the summit while a buzzing hissed in her ears. She had known dread, now it was hunger, and the fear of a lonely death. Suddenly, her heart stopped. Suddenly, before her was Shiva.

Shiva had his back to her, sitting immobile in a perfect lotus position, his hair twisted in a knot atop his head. "Here is the fire that drew me in," Reshma thought, without noticing the hunk of fatty meat roasting over it. "I have climbed the Kailash to where the Lord resides, in the very heart of the Mountain. When the sun rises, I will find his tiger skin in a thicket near here, along with his two-headed damaru." Lost in the vision, she didn't notice that the meditating athlete had shifted slightly. His body was still, but his profile was turned towards her. He glanced at her. Reshma had already dropped to her knees, reciting chants of praise. Trying his best not to laugh he decided to play along.

"The world is beautiful," he murmured in honeyed tones, "for her who is the mistress of her body and mind."

Reshma dissolved in gratitude and, with eyes closed, raised her face towards him. Gazing directly upon him would have dazzled her.

"What we mean by 'happiness' is the cessation of struggle, isn't that so, young lady?" the god went on, with calculated persuasion. "So don't struggle, my beloved."

Had she heard right? Around them, nature and the night conspired to amplify his message. It was warm, a breeze gently stirred the trees. No wild boar grunted coarsely or rustled in the bushes.

"Do not be surprised to see me in human form," Shiva added, leaning towards Reshma's upraised face. "But your limited human intelligence prevents it being otherwise. Very well then, worship me in the guise of a man."

It seemed to him that she was about to melt in acquiescence. Pleased with his joke, the young athlete burst out laughing and the jig was up. Reshma straightened herself. Shocked, then blushing and angry, she jerked her veil tight around her, about to flee. A large hand came down on her wrist. They looked each other in the eye: he radiant, she wild. Touched by her innocence, he looked again, with respect, and went to sit on a stone a few steps away, to give her time to collect herself.

"My name is Chuharmal. Can you forgive me?" he asked, simply.

They spoke for hours, their voices weaving together

as if their souls flowed towards each other. Reshma brought breath and life to everything she touched, and Chuharmal loved her because he sensed the love in her.

She explained where she was from and alluded to her sisters, who were on their way to Mahisautha.

"The Malins are filled with the spirit of flowers," she said softly. "They are unrivalled at painting nature."

"Do you understand the language of animals?" Chuharmal asked.

She tipped her head. "Of parrots? When they repeat that..."

"... Desire chains us to the wheel of rebirth," he finished her sentence in a serious voice.

In fact, a pair of parrots had alighted near them as their desire for love grew, but they didn't see the wreath of green flames the birds lit in the darkness.

"My sisters, Dauna and Kushuma will be living at the court of your uncle, King Somdev, your cousins' father," Reshma went on, pensively. "But I must go to Pakaria. Will I ever see my sisters again?"

Chuharmal looked bewildered. "Of what cousins do you speak?"

"Of Jaybhardan, Moti Ram and Budeshwar. Were you not aware of their existence? They say that Jaybhardan is destined to do great things," she added.

An inexplicable sadness darkened Chuharmal's eyes and stabbed at his heart. Why should another's claim to greatness affect him so? He swept the question aside with an impatient wave, and the sky of his soul descended.

Had he, Chuharmal, done anything so terrible in the past that its consequences assigned him to mediocrity? Red feathers and green flames! What kind of night was this? Then he saw his companion's beauty and her ardent gaze, and hugged Reshma tight to him, so to become one with her.

In the morning, both found that the tasks their elders had assigned them were an unbearable prospect. Why ever should Reshma go all the way to Pakaria if Chuharmal wasn't there? What was the point of slaving over a statue of Hanuman for someone who had no talent or taste for handicrafts?

"We'll go to Princess Chandravati together," the young woman heard herself say, her mind made up. "And as for the statue of Hanuman, let me take care of that."

"How will you manage it?" Chuharmal asked, amused at her aplomb.

"Shiva blessed us last night," Reshma replied breathlessly. "Look."

She pointed to the ground where they had slept: the earth their bodies had seeded was broken, as if under the hooves of the sacred bull.

"All I have to do is take a bit of this. I'll mix in some plants whose secrets I know, and use the clay to mould the statue. Once it's dry, painting Hanuman will be child's play."

Chuharmal realized that the love of such a woman would unfurl a strength of its own. Once the statue had been placed in the arena, and his debt towards Bhima was repaid, he could leave with her and serve Chandravati. He would get King Bhim Sain to appoint him a watchman over the garden of Pakaria. Him, and no other.

"May your wish come true," Reshma whispered, dazzled by the bearing of the man who had taken her hand.

9

While everyone in the king's court was satisfied with Moti Ram's, Budeshwar's and Karikant's progress, the courtiers found Jaybhardan deeply annoying. The prince had a mind of his own. Somdev, himself an intrigued onlooker, replied enigmatically to anyone who complained: "My son does novel things." Jaybhardan had turned the park in Mahisautha into an experimental field; he ploughed it like a peasant, and except for marking the sacrificial rites, spent less time in the temple than his father. Those who presumed to urge marriage to him were promptly sent packing. One day, at Somdev's suggestion that he get some practice in oratory, he stepped atop a box placed before the royal sal and upset the assembly of knights by declaring that henceforth the duties transmitted from father to son should be handled by "responsible" men. No one understood. As for Somdev, he just smiled.

Jaybhardan expressed a desire to build huts for the palace servants, whom no one had yet imagined needing a roof of their own to dwell, eat or sleep under. His elephants had been tasked with clearing the land: knocking down trees, trampling, digging and levelling—it had all been most impressive.

Of course, the tender shoots of ornamental plants were also trampled, but Somdev was so proud of the great beasts he let them get away with anything. Bhuranand was inseparable from Jaybhardan, close as a shadow. The prince only ever travelled on foot or elephant-back, adamantly refusing to use a sedan chair. He spoke little, his gaze lost in the distance, no one knew where. In his presence, Somdev rarely did more than bob his head in agreement. The frustrated courtiers brooded, all the more bitterly in that Jaybhardan had started holding forth on "the necessity of educating children". Someone had even heard him talk of including the sons of mahouts and bricklayers—whom the knights called "the dregs of the earth".

They had been watching Somdev keenly. Given the king's ridiculous indulgence, his eldest son was sure to establish a grotesque form of government. They had to get the young man sent away and keep the senile old sovereign on the throne for as long as possible.

Apart from nursing personal grievances against a prince bent on poking holes in their privileges, the knights lambasted him for two suspicious characteristics: first of all, Jaybhardan spoke much too gently, even to his elephant, the soles and nails of whose feet he insisted on tending to himself. And he was worryingly self-assured.

A gentle voice. Worrisome self-assurance.

▼

Somdev knew his son's heart. Jaybhardan's words were charged with the original force of unspoilt humankind: to him, thinking, saying, and accomplishing were of a piece. No gap, no loss. His rectitude never weakened, nor did his senses go astray. The Brahmins came close to admitting that a trace of divine freedom seemed to gleam within him: the guru had awakened him to the infinite nature of his character. That would explain the irresistible attraction he held for people of all ages and from all walks of life. Graced with such a son, Somdev had the satisfaction of knowing that the world he would leave behind held reflected glimpses of celestial splendour. In the meantime, he was old and wise enough to keep a watchful eye on his court. Although the people were fond of Jaybhardan, it was still too soon to hand all power over to him. Or the knights would have him atone for the sin of his existence as harshly as if he had stolen a holy man's cow.

"People's cynicism will be his downfall," the king was telling his advisor, yet again.

"Then send him away from court, your majesty. He will come back battered and bruised, but stronger."

His power comes from the heart and from his cosmic affinities, Somdev realized while pondering certain alchemical formulae. Because it emanates from the original substance of the universe, it cannot be corrupted. When combined with wisdom, his innocence is his supreme power.

"You're right, my friend," he eventually replied. "Jaybhardan must go beyond the borders of the kingdom to be toughened up."

▼

Jaybhardan had received a well-rounded education, like his brothers and his nephew, Karikant. Nonetheless, from a young age, he had refused to hunt. The refusal had exposed him to mockery, but since he excelled with the bow and arrow, the critics were foiled. His archery master even compared him to the ambidextrous Arjuna. "Once the anguish of life and the fear of death have been dissolved, you will be unreachable," the admiring master was given to saying.

A few knights also bowed to him, impressed by his example. Knowing that a heart at peace made one indestructible, they begged to know his secret.

"Meditate, draw the bow, and shoot the arrow in your mind. Nothing more," he replied sincerely.

For all that, everyone agreed Jaybhardan was turning into a risk for the stability of the kingdom.

To oust him from Mahisautha, the wicked began spreading strange rumours about him. First, the wet nurses said that when he was born, the night ran away from the day, and a bit of time had gone missing ever since. The result was that the calculations of astrologers had been thrown off. The wet nurses also told an incredible story against the midwife who had attended his birth. Her name was Urmila, and they said she was even more unclean than the rest of her kind.

"May the Son of the Wind dry her husk and scatter it!" they cried. "The woman claims that Jaybhardan wanted to be born again, to grow inside another body—this when his mother was queen! What's more, he wanted to do this in the womb of a Chandala, a dog-eater, some pauperess like herself! The vile nag made it up, of course... Wretch that she is, she insists it's true. She says he wanted to be reborn outside the courtly circle, among the Untouchables! That the prince, not long ago, had shrunk himself back to an embryonic state in order to be reborn amongst the poorest of the poor. She even adds that he won his brothers over to the plan. May the gods wreak her downfall and throw her in five pieces to the crocodiles!"

The wet nurses had an explanation for everything. Jaybhardan had run into an impoverished pregnant woman in the forest during the previous lunar cycle. In the throes of labour, she was moaning because her offspring would be condemned to a life of blows, to being spat upon and scorned like her.

"The Chandalin was crying her heart out. Jaybhardan began the kind of speech he's used to making under the sal. He wanted to offer her some dignity, if you please. As though our fates weren't already decided by our birth! Nor did he stop here. He and his brothers performed magic. All three shrank themselves until they were small enough to replace the contemptible runt in the Chandalin's womb, and then she delivered them with the help of the midwife."

So it came to pass that the sons of the royal couple were birthed a second time by a vile, despicable woman, and those who told the tale emphasized that that precisely had been Jaybhardan's intention: to be reborn amongst the dregs of the earth.

When he learned of the scandal, the Brahmin summoned the prince post-haste. He waited for him outside the temple, a silhouette of rage framed by two broad pillars. The scantily clad young man stood straight as a lance before him. "The vile and the dregs are of the same divine essence as gold, as are Brahmins and pigs, the lotus flower and the smelly mulch whence it grows," he declared to the Brahmin, who blanched in horror. "A royal womb and a lowly one are equal, I can assure you, and the experience of being born from them is the same. You teach Divine Oneness: observe that I believe in it absolutely."

The Brahmin collected his thoughts, hesitated briefly, then bowed to Jaybhardan, not out of guile, but because his soul was moved.

The courtiers exiled the midwife, and prayed that the wolves would rid them of her. Later there were rumours that she had been abused by a brigand and had sought refuge on the Mountain. Somdev got wind of the embryo story. It plunged him into an abyss of reflection, but his attitude towards his son barely changed, which thickened still more the atmosphere of mystery around them in the palace.

The tale spread across the plains and along the valleys and even climbed the foothills of the Himalayas, where it brought solace to many miserable people who had not yet dared challenge their own reality. No one knew what had happened to the midwife the wet nurses had called a dog-eater; but everyone knew that the prince and his brothers continued to visit families cast into violence and filth. To anyone in Mahisautha who referred to the scandal, Jaybhardan replied that the forest had initiated him into the Revolution of Love, and this revolution would spread far and wide. He spoke of sharing, of looks and gestures measured with respect, of simply paying attention. Above all, paying attention to other beings.

10

The embryo story sent imaginations reeling across the country, even infecting populations halfway up the Mountain, but back in the guru's cave, the prince remained tight-lipped about the whole affair. The old man couldn't let it go. The subject raised essential issues, but how could he introduce it into their lessons? Should he start with a paradox? Say to his pupils, for instance, "A human being's reality is spiritual first and foremost, and yet he springs from a tiny speck of physical matter, how do you reconcile that?" No, that would take too long, when there was just one question he was itching to ask, "Jaybhardan, did you or did you not manage to return to the state of an embryo?"

The rest hardly bothered him. He was confident in the idea of the continuity of forms among the living, from the humblest to the most high-ranking, and a prince's body passing through an Untouchable's did not shock him in the least. Change was part of life, and nature had the means at her disposal.

He could have brandished "caste duty" before Somdev's heir, as everyone else did, but in the end, he opted for a different approach:

"So, my boy, speak frankly: is it acceptable for midwives to be singled out for disgust, as though they wallowed in uncleanliness, when what they serve is sacred life?"

Jaybhardan nodded slowly, to show that he appreciated the question, but he didn't take the bait. His face remained still, his gaze wide. His companions followed his example as best they could. The scent of betel hung heavily in the den, and the guru had to hold back a sigh.

"Every matrix is indeed sacred, my boys," he commenced, prudently. "And that isn't true only of wombs and birth canals. At whatever point one becomes absorbed in the universe, the Divine Whole reveals itself. Every point in the universe is a centre... The mystery of the centre!"

Turning to face Moti Ram, Budeshwar and Karikant, he went on, "So tell me... Where would your centre be, if you had to choose one?"

"The heart, master," all three boys replied in unison, their faces polished by the light of a torch suspended from the rock.

The guru assented, then turned and drove his gaze directly into the eyes of the eldest, who barely lowered his eyelids.

"Penetrate deeply into your heart, Jaybhardan. Put yourself fully into the situation. Into the state, I mean. What escaped through your senses is contracting and becoming concentrated, withdrawing from the world and gathering itself. Yes, all of your energy is gathering... Is it well compressed? As big as nothing and as serious as the universe?"

With eyes half closed, the young man seemed to pull his presence in, away from them. The light became more intense, caressing his forehead, the ridge of his cheekbones where they met his fine eyes, and the bridge of his somewhat long nose.

"Plenitude or vacuum, at the intersection!" a host of Invisibles clamoured round. "At the poles, energy gathers itself and takes root in the eternal."

The old guru cleared his throat and changed his tone. "You have reached a-temporality and a-causality, haven't you?" he insinuated. "The Real is in the centre. No more contingencies. No more limitations: you don't feel yourself any more, you don't worry about wondering if you are identical to your body or your mind. So tell me whether or not everything is possible in the centre?"

The prince brought his hands together. Was he or wasn't he going to spit it out at last? The guru's piercing eye rolled from one corner to the other. The old man pressed on, not worrying about the other three any longer. "One moment a giant, the next, an embryo..."

Jaybhardan smiled gracefully, but didn't say a word. The other sniffed in vexation, and spat out, his forehead furrowed, "The Real and the True vibrate at their intersection, everything is there, and you are with it. You don't know which way it will go, inwards or outwards... You are at the point of equilibrium, where everything is equal. But it doesn't last. Everything will accelerate."

No matter how he plumbed and probed his prince, the young man was imperturbable. His best disciple ever. What level of consciousness had the precocious young fellow attained?

The young man let his words slip softly towards his teacher and, in an almost inaudible voice, said, "In the centre, consciousness and energy coincide at a point that draws the entire universe into itself."

Yes, yes, that's it, the guru mused. Let's wait for what comes next.

"Then, the polar end projects towards the exterior, whatever karma allows for. This is where strength of character is expressed."

The guru was amazed. Excellent, his pupil was truly excellent. Suddenly, realizing he had been thwarted, he spat out in exasperation, "Let's get to the point, Jaybhardan. Are you trying to drive me crazy? The midwife, this Urmila woman... Everyone is telling wild stories about you all over the place. But speak to me; I'll believe you. Tell me the truth."

He was practically begging now, not even bothering to hide his desperation.

"So, what happened? Was it a witch's spell, or the manifestation of divine generosity? Is Jaybhardan capable of compressing the powers of the universe to such an extreme that he can render them in a phenomenal way... in *his own* way?"

The prince's eyes went frosty. He crossed his hands beneath his chin, suddenly distant. The guru lost his composure, "Are you capable of producing an earthly phenomenon from the powers of the universe? Are you? Of transmutations? Materializations? Tell me, damn it! Are you capable of planting yourself as an embryo in a woman's womb?"

The old man cared only about the magic. That was it. He paid no attention to his pupil's decision to be a bridge between the "Untouchables" and the rest of society. A shadow passed over Jaybhardan. Without meaning to, the grasping old man had just taught him one last lesson: displaying your gifts was risky for adepts of the mystical way. The temptation of claiming powers was too great.

The guru knew he had disappointed his pupil. He muttered to himself and gave up. "Time will tell how powerful you are, Jaybhardan, and how far your abilities stretch," he concluded in a trembling voice, with a vague fluttering of his hand.

His disciples saw his eyes searching for his bag of betel as he muttered incomprehensibly, his beard twisting and coiling on his chest. The young men were about to prostrate themselves at his feet when he suddenly sat up straight for one final declaration, puny and superb, draped in white, his tongue slapping. "Your liberation, young men! Go for it, for goodness' sake. Knead matter to its essence! Emancipate yourselves, my odd little boys!"

Gutted, he slumped into a pile of rags on the floor, sobbing like a child.

"No woman ever rolled my betel leaf and stuck a clove into it," he whined, "none ever sprinkled it with cardamom or ground acacia bark. Not one woman has ever prepared it for me. Ah! Follow your path as best you can, but take care to provision yourselves with happiness."

The Invisibles vanished one by one, whispering their dismay. A discreet flurry filled the cave. To his companions—spellbound by the red hues streaking their guru's face—Jaybhardan shot a reassuring glance. He leaned over and placed his hand lightly on the old man's shoulder.

"Great master, you speak true," he whispered, overcome with emotion, kneeling before what was now no more than a white haze. "Freedom is our vocation. We will achieve it by working selflessly. We wish neither to forge new chains for ourselves, nor make them for others."

11

The guru's death coincided with Dauna and Kushuma's arrival. Somdev had asked Jaybhardan to welcome them in front of the Shiva temple in the woods. Victory, the divine trident, was glittering in the sunlight, veiled at moments by the leaves, at others so dazzlingly bright as scarcely to be visible to the human eye. The prince arrived at the site early enough to be able to say a brief prayer. "Accept, Shiva, that I purify my voice by reciting your poems. So I may not waste it on futile things."

Since Jaybhardan was early, he went for a stroll in the woods, following the flight of the turtledoves and bulbuls. And so it came to pass that he overheard a conversation among his companions. They were horsing around behind a copse, and laughing about the knights, the ancestors and Jaybhardan's cosmic debt, the social faux pas that no one could forgive in the palace, the prince's refusal to abide by his caste duty. Their talk turned to the bawdiness that sullied the halls of the throne room, and they threw jabs at the heir who had no taste for the "alley of pleasure".

Jaybhardan recognized Moti Ram's ringing laughter, and was overcome with emotion. Even exile would be preferable to a wedding that might weaken him. He took the Lord as his witness: yes, freedom was his vocation, and yes, liberating others his duty—the method would come later. His brothers could decide for themselves.

Instinctively, he raised his eyes to the tops of the sal trees. Several of them were wasting away, some already dead, their bases lacerated at some two cubits from the ground, their bark slashed into rings. Bhuranand was without blame, he didn't eat sal bark.

"The mating season is coming," Jaybhardan thought coldly. "The bucks' heads itch; they come here to be rid of their antlers. Death and love truly go hand in hand."

The prince plumbed his own heart. He saw himself as an infant, then as a toddler, his skull shaved for the ceremony with the astrologer. The barber had shown everyone assembled the single lock spared by his blade, while his aunt gathered the hair that had fallen into a cloth bag filled with flour. His aunt joined the cortege of women chanting traditional hymns behind his mother, Queen Madoderi, and the image faded away. Next he saw his sister, Bansapti, preparing the sacred cord for him. It marked the end of his childhood, and his entrance into the world of men, the world of caste. He saw himself on the cusp of his second existence, alone with his beloved father for their first meal... Those images faded in turn, and were replaced by the Luminaries, lightning bursting through their uncertain light. Songs of propitiation to Indra, the God of the Elements, rose up, dying out softly. He saw the guru standing before him, his wrinkled old hands waving the symbols of the sadhu, those who have renounced worldly life: the saffron robes and the pilgrim's staff. The image shimmered over the Ganga. Then it, too, faded away.

"There is much that is good in our traditions," Jaybhardan thought, "but we should liberate ourselves from them. I will not renounce the world. On the contrary, I will devote myself to working in it to help both boys and girls find their own paths. Neither a sadhu nor a spouse shall I be! May I be at the Lord's disposal."

Between the sight of his brothers' delight in farcical amusements and the thought of the Malins who were about to arrive, he was overwhelmed by annoyance. "Our servants will collect the two sisters and lead them to the wing of the palace reserved for women," he announced sternly. "We are going back." Surprised by his mood and the change of plans, Karikant ventured to ask, "What about Shiva? We were supposed to show the Malins the parts of his temple that need repainting..."

"Shiva doesn't need a coat of paint," Jaybhardan shot back. "Shiva doesn't need anything from anyone. We shall act as though he didn't exist. We'll be close enough to the truth."

He immured himself in silence, gnawed by a fierce sadness he couldn't explain. "Shiva doesn't exist." Was that where all his years of study had led him?

That evening, prepared for a well-deserved reprimand, he sought Somdev out rather than awaiting his summons. He was still in the grip of anger.

"Those girls from Madhubani can repaint Shiva's temple if that is your will, Father, but know that I wash my hands of the whole business. Why did you summon them here? Why must there be art? Creating illusion! Do we so doubt the divine presence that we feel the need to illustrate it? Are the heavens and my father trying to pen me in a trap?"

The king pursed his lips. Jaybhardan went on, vehemently, his scalp flushed, a loose lock of hair waving like a standard, "Art leads the mind towards idleness by suffocating it in material things. By seducing the senses, it captures the mind and impedes it from encountering the subtle."

"My son is being excessive," Somdev replied sternly. "The Malins' flowers are said to be admirable."

Jaybhardan flared up, "Father, no matter how genial those girls may be, will their art allow us to glimpse the source from which it springs?"

Somdev let a long silence pass, during which he scanned his son. A tremor crossed Somdev's face. Jaybhardan started to step back, but the king laid a soothing hand on his arm.

"Let us not harden our hearts, my dear son. Dauna and Kushuma faced the dangers of a long journey to come to us. Let us welcome them properly."

"Father, don't ask me again," Jaybhardan replied, arms crossed over his chest. "A premonition warns me against it."

"Now, now," Somdev whispered. "What might that be?"

The words spilled out of Jaybhardan too quickly, his gaze still transfixed by the vision of the dead trees spoiling the stream of green horizons. "A premonition of love. Love makes us lose our heads, I've heard."

Somdev shook his head in disapproval. Jaybhardan burst out, "But Father, magical women!"

"My son is filled with contradictions," the king replied without looking at him. "What happened to his speeches about the great reality? Lord! Remove the vain and pretentious, unable to embrace mindfulness, from my sight."

Was his sadness feigned? Jaybhardan drew closer, his tears brimming, "Allow me to leave Mahisautha, Father, I beg of you. By your leave, I will be gone tomorrow."

"Very well," Somdev replied, his face impenetrable, eyelids lowered. "You will take Bhuranand and a few servants. Sleep on it, by morning you will know where to go." He added, "Bhuranand, and all the elephants of Mahisautha."

Jaybhardan made arrangements with the mahouts and his servants, before informing his brothers and nephew of his departure. They were distraught. They chose to follow him, and took an oath of fealty. He embraced them warmly and asked them to wait while he went to the time-worn Shiva temple in the woods.

"Lord Shiva," he prayed, "deliver me from emotions. Krishna's words resound in me unceasingly: 'Faced with the ineluctable, you must not pity yourself.' Impermanent and powerless, I want to entrust you with my soul, cleansed of all low feelings, as Arjuna entrusted his to Krishna."

He thought he glimpsed the white silhouette of the

bull Nandi, Shiva's mount. "Vanity of art," escaped his lips.

A loud hooting, not far, trailed off into a moan. Jaybhardan bowed until his head touched the ground before the edifice. The entrance, four steps framed by thick columns, looked like the gaping mouth of a monstrous head. At the back, in place of a glottis, he could see the statue of a stocky god bedecked in jewellery.

"Tiger skin, ashes, and serpent!" he implored in silence. "I am driving the mirror of the senses away from myself. I come to you from where I was born, and search for you within myself."

The wind picked up instantly, expelled from the thousand nostrils of night, knocking him down; it set him rolling over the ground.

"Darkness! Accursed darkness!" Jaybhardan cried out, the back of his neck pinned beneath an invisible knee. "Remove your clawing tendrils from me!"

A whirlwind whipped the ten directions of space. Nestling into his own death, he saw his clothes, with his flesh inside, floating far away, like bits of clouds.

"Oh, Lord! Why do you dance on my skull? What can you tear from one whose existence is barely begun? Already have I detached myself from down here, and no longer have a home."

After a while, the green shoots of the sal trees murmured in his ears, "Are you free of fear?"

The wind grazed the crest of a new dawn, reaching over the divine architecture. Gods and goddesses stopped short of the great origin. The prince finally understood: he had offended their king by granting himself a forbidden power. He had raised himself to the level of Indra, father of Arjuna and forefather of Shiva, known for inserting himself into wombs of his choosing.

"Ancient laws separated humanity into scornful or hostile groups," he argued. "Isn't that unjust and unworthy? See the entire universe in me, O Supreme Spirit and Lord of all beings. I am at your mercy."

Astride Airavata, the three-headed elephant, Indra grasped the firmament and drew back the rainbow. He shot an arrow that burst open a mountain of clouds overhead, showering the prince in a seminal rain.

2

1

From clouds passing low over the earth, the gods peered down to see how human affairs were progressing. Afterwards, they gathered in a circle to consult with one another.

"I like this prince," said Krishna. "He reminds of a young Arjuna."

The others concurred heartily. Krishna added, "I think he's made a good start on the path to renunciation: concentration, meditation, contemplative concentration... What do you think, Shiva?"

"The son of Somdev is a long way from achieving supreme peace," Shiva observed. "He is, however, brave enough to stand up to the courtiers. He transgresses, he frees himself from the conditions imposed on him... He grasps that the distinction between beings exists solely in how far the expansion of Oneness is realized by each one. He will be opposed by ignorance and passion, but he won't yield to them."

The gods assented.

"Jaybhardan, the son of King Somdev of Mahisautha, has made himself the champion of the humble," Shiva added, opening all of his eyes at once to gaze upon the Earth. "At my side, he will destroy appearances and false categories. Provisional arrangements will yield to the revelation of the essential nature of all beings. He will surpass Arjuna, because the state of the world calls for him. I acknowledge him as my beloved son. He will be king among the Luminous. King of the Mountain. Your turn, Krishna."

"The prince is the best among yogis," he murmured, leaning into the endless sky. "The best both for his mastery of vital energy and for his knowledge... But let him not bind himself to extreme constraint."

"Such moderation, Krishna!" Shiva exclaimed. "But look again at the rider who is one with the elephant. He who worships the absolute through me will dissolve into me."

2

In the section of the palace that had been reserved for them, the girls from Madhubani were a close-knit group. Six Maithils in all, they had just caught a glimpse of Somdev's sons, and were dying to catch their eye. They began to fear the arrival of Dauna and Kushuma, whose beauty was sure to have blossomed. What if the Malins swayed the king and he charged them with depicting the Ashok Vatika, in addition to doing the pillars? As far as they were concerned, the Ashok Vatika was the treasure of the *Ramayana*, the garden where the demon-king Ravana had imprisoned Sita. It symbolized women's lives: it symbolized waiting for a man. Through Sita, wrongly suspected of infidelity by Rama, they shared in advance the chafing loneliness of every wife in the world whose fate lay in the hands of a fallible man. Why were men always wary of women's love?

Despite the dire warning of the saga's climax, the Maithils couldn't help admiring Somdev's sons and were already praising Jaybhardan to the skies: Jaybhardan the standard-bearer of generous humanity, forced into exile like the hero, but who, unlike Rama, had left without marrying.

Dauna and Kushuma arrived, and were soon introduced to the Maithils. The first evening went without a hitch. But in the morning, one of the girls from Madhubani whispered to her sisters, "The Malins spoke of Jaybhardan in their sleep. Not of Ravana, nor of those who hide in flying fortresses to battle the gods. Of Jaybhardan. He was dressed in a never-seen-before shade of blue, one that no monsoon could fade, nor even cow's urine."

"The blue hidden in the tiniest vein of an elephant's ear?" one curious girl asked. "In Shiva's throat? In Krishna's body?"

"Beware repugnant indigo," the last girl commented. "The blue of the lower classes and that of extreme power always catch the eye of women."

▼

Dauna and Kushuma were so close that the beauty of one was reflected in the other, its force shuttling between them, so that passing people would often think they had seen a single charming person. The two even had their feelings in common.

When morning came, they wandered among the flower-beds surrounding the palace, seeking the plants they needed to prepare colours. The weather was pleasant and mild, and by noon the sisters were as deeply lost in abstraction as if it were twilight.

"He came, didn't he?" Kushuma asked, plopping herself down in the shade of a neem tree.

"Yes," said Dauna, as she came to sit next to her sister. "Arjuna came in the guise of Prince Jaybhardan... He was garbed in blue."

"With a touch of orange," added Kushuma, pensively.

"Our ancestor's soul left its hiding place to descend into the body of the son of Somdev," Dauna went on, her eyes half closed. "That soul is becoming incarnated; now it is up to Prince Jaybhardan to rise towards his divine nature."

"Such a moving dream we had..." Kushuma murmured, tipping her head to one side. "Tell me, dear sister, neem blossoms are male and become female, don't they? But what gender are magicians?"

"I don't know what to think any more," Dauna answered, her voice trailing off. "Do you see Prince Jaybhardan?"

"Am I female?" Kushuma asked breathily, as she drifted into sleep. "I see him heading towards a lake with an elephant of immeasurable size. What a strange sensation, sister... It's as though I wished to become one with the prince."

"Then am I, too, female?" Dauna echoed her.

From that point on, the urge to meet Jaybhardan gave them no respite. It was hunger and thirst, fierce and painful. Its turbulence disordered their humours, while the world's violence pierced their entrails. They forgot that their bodies were no more than a minuscule frame for eternal love, and began to worship a man whom they had yet to meet.

If they asked where Jaybhardan took his elephants for a bath, Somdev's servants would reply with a shrug, "Of which heir do you speak? The one who was once so devoted to archery left with his brothers yesterday."

Yet, they set off without a moment's hesitation, walking beneath the trees he had cherished. In their branches, monkeys with round eyes hugged their females, and bird couples drew closer together in the foliage. The Invisibles shooed the shadows away, and the sal trees parted to reveal the temple where the prince liked to meditate. Shiva's female form rode her tiger, glittering in the fiery air.

"The goddess of war!" Kushuma shrieked in terror. "Jaybhardan is in danger. Let us throw him sacred herbs!"

"Had we ten horses to offer him, they would be as useless as a rice pudding," Dauna replied, trembling. "We must think, sister, I pray you. The goddess has shown herself to us, we are the ones she is testing. She has shown us her weapons. She wants us to seize them and overcome our passions, I am sure of it."

As though drawn away by a two-headed drum, the feathery clouds were sucked to the bottom of the sky, which shaped them into a translucent spiral.

"The sign of supreme perfection!" Kushuma stammered, her heart pounding in her chest. "Shall we follow it, Dauna?"

"If our minds can hold out against our senses," her sister replied, still trembling.

She stretched out her arm and pointed. "The lake of lotuses is that way. If death lies at the bottom, it shall cover us with the white shroud of men or the red shroud of women."

3

Bhuranand was waiting for Jaybhardan by the river. They were to join their travelling companions as Mahisautha faded behind the dusty horde. The servants were handling the final preparations for departure. Jaybhardan urged them on.

"Lord Shiva, the universe filled with your secret reveals only an infinitesimal bit," he intoned, his face raised, the triple mark of the god on his forehead. "May the day come when I dissolve into your silent vision."

He entrusted his tunic to a fifteen-year-old boy named Anil, who was acting as his aide-de-camp. When he leaned over the lake to greet the face of his youth one last time, he saw blood pearling on the white lines traced by the edge of the divine axe, three dripping trails that soon stained the water red. The prince leapt back. The axe spun in space and landed on his skull. The line parting his great mass of hair opened in a bloody gash.

"What alliance is this between thyself and me?" he exclaimed, flustered. "Am I a woman? The word shatters the screen of thy many forms, Lord Shiva! May I be worthy to bow before them all, including ones yet incomprehensible to me. May I heed their warnings."

The vermilion water went still for an instant and the image disappeared. The prince plunged his hand in, and it was coloured with the traditional sindhoor. His feelings began to flow out, released into the water until there was nothing left. For a single second, or a thousand times less, he was freed from them. "The Lord's time is a thousand aeons, and a thousand aeons his night." The ancient words swirled in his head before vanishing.

Awareness of his breath returned to him gradually. He was near the lake. Anil was bowing to him, with his tunic over his heart. A few feet away, Moti Ram and Budeshwar were enjoying saffron-rice cakes with the others.

▼

The mahouts had finished grooming the elephants when Bhuranand raised the alarm. Jaybhardan and his brothers heard him trumpeting, and soon saw a distraught messenger from Somdev running towards them, hair combed by the wind.

"Prince of the forests and ponds," the man said, bowing low before Jaybhardan, "it is too soon for exile. The invaders have returned. Mahisautha is under attack, or will be tomorrow. We must go into battle."

Dumbstruck, Jaybhardan didn't reply. His brothers had been similarly stunned into silence.

"They are about to enter our territory," the king's messenger added, straightening up. "From what we can tell, they mean to pillage our lands and the neighbouring countries to the east. They'll run their weapons through the women and children. The bark of the sal trees will be lacquered with gore."

Jaybhardan's face was inscrutable. "All roles are noble," he was thinking, "as long as one is in his proper place. Where is mine?"

"King Somdev has summoned the head of his army, who will put as many men as necessary at your disposal," the man went on feverishly. "Our sovereign believes that Muzaffarpur will come to our aid. Darbhanga and Madhubani too."

"Muzaffarpur, Madhubani..." Moti Ram and Budeshwar echoed, taken aback.

"There was no question of the slightest danger yesterday," Karikant wondered, glancing with concern at Jaybhardan, whose look was impenetrable, then swivelled to regard emissary's betel-spattered pouch. "Are you sure of what you're saying?"

The man explained that a female spy disguised as a rat-eater had arrived the night before. Pretending to be a beggar she had approached the king, who was always kind to beggars. The spy had reminded him of someone, he couldn't say whom. She informed him that she had dashed down the Mountain keeping just ahead of the Chinese, whose numbers were swelling by the day.

The emissary seemed confused. His overheated brain was a steaming kettle of panic, enemy hordes bubbling out of every orifice.

"Calm down, my good friend," said Jaybhardan. "The great Harshvardhana fought to enlarge his supremacy, and we never blamed him for it. We will fulfil the duties of our birth and our role in the world, without judging others. I will examine my soul to discern where my duty lies. What did Somdev say?"

"Our father is no warmonger," Moti Ram snapped, cutting him off.

"Reinforcing his defences has always sufficed," Budeshwar added.

They all knew that Jaybhardan was endowed with a discernment they often lacked; in his turn he listened willingly to them. "Between the three brothers, you unite the light, the shadow, and the darkness, my dear boys," their guru used to say, when in a mood to show them some affection. "When I look at you, I see the virtues of nature in balance. Alas, men require action, the poor things, it's inevitable. Train your spirit to distinguish itself, that is all I ask: march straight and don't be attached to the outcome." He would punctuate his statements with the sharp nod that Moti Ram and Budeshwar would mimic when he wasn't looking.

"I think my grandfather is trying to make a point," Karikant commented thoughtfully.

Jaybhardan smiled and invited the emissary to sit with them.

"Have something to eat, my good man, and speak frankly. Are the Chinese really marching on Mahisautha?"

The emissary looked up, startled.

"With the most ferocious warriors from both the north and the south," he tossed out fiercely.

"Eat your fill and go back to the king," the prince addressed him, perfectly calm now. "We have not yet left Somdev's lands. We are at his service."

▼

As soon as they reached the deserted lake, Dauna declared that a ceremony had taken place on the shore.

"Heaven and earth attest to it, Kushuma," she confirmed. "Whether Jaybhardan has garbed himself in the linen shirt, embroidered robes, woollen shawl and cloak of royalty matters not. I speak of an initiation. In this place, Jaybhardan crossed the threshold to a different kingdom."

Kushuma looked up at her with inquiring eyes, but her gaze was caught by birds flitting through the branches of the trees, and she responded only with peals of laughter before diving into the water.

"May my body enjoy the cool water that has touched his," she exclaimed.

"I aspire to know the beauty of his spirit," Dauna murmured uncertainly, entering the water in turn.

Abruptly, birds in great numbers flocked overhead, flocks of the kind the women of Mithila drew to symbolize carnal desire. The pair of sisters stopped trying to control their senses, and forgot what the Book of Fate had planned for them, even their mother's recommendations and those of the priests who knew about thresholds and limits between day and night. Their splashing had raised the sindhoor left in the water. When they stepped out of the water, they saw that the parting in their hair had turned vermilion and the symbols of marriage had been set upon them. They lay on the ground and covered themselves with jasmine blossoms that turned into jewellery, their emblems as married women, and their lips parted to call Jaybhardan.

4

At a window of the palace, Somdev had some kusha herbs burned, their sacred scent floated to the sky. The smoke curled into the dust rising in the courtyard. Beneath him, horses clad in armour awaited the spurs of the cavalrymen. In the distance, the summit of Mount Meru vanished into the clouds.

Jaybhardan noticed a soldier nearby, about the same age as he, who was busy dressing his steed's hooves with oil. Had they ever spoken? Spoken and understood each other? The prince hesitated, trying to place this familiar stranger. His gaze tired from watching him, while the soldier's absorption belied the improbable, martial character of such an activity being carried out in the royal enclosure. His repetitive movements drew in the edifices, the landscapes and the men, brought them all converging on a precise focal point. The entire scene plunged into the mirrored surface of the hoof, reduced to a contrast, a flash of white light on the horny hoof wall, then a band wholly black. Jaybhardan blinked. Must he go to fight, impale, shatter, and behead? Must he grow enraged, make himself a hyena or a jackal, and bring his fellow men to their last gasp? He had been raised to respect the *Gita* and the role models his father held up to him, fully aware of the prescribed duties of his high birth, his caste. But his mind was filled with the first story of the world, the one that transcends history and has made non-violence the energy of the cosmic order. Violence accompanied mistakes and misunderstanding, but love was the fulfilment of truth. This fact had grown in him to the point of obsession.

"Mahisautha is not the battlefield of Kuru, Father," he said to Somdev. "You know that in my eyes, the Great Battle is not against the Chinese soldiers. The one in my mind resembles the stone for grinding grains, stone on stone, stick and hole, motion and stillness testing each other."

"This contest, like the unceasing battle between health and disease, will also be fought between the world and you, my son," Somdev finished his thought.

Emotion overran Jaybhardan's heart and burst out.

"Why did you call me back, Father?" he cried. "You have your army. Many men and horses. Take back the elephants you gave me, the servants, young Anil. Keep your sons, my brothers. Moti Ram will be your chief commander; he will be your heir. I seek the founding principles of the universe and aim for the ultimate goal. Do not expect martial brutality from me. Do not ask me to disembowel another."

Somdev's eyes narrowed.

"You are of the heroic caste of warriors," the king returned. "Your duty is here and now. What do you seek to avoid? Rather, accomplish what must be accomplished in the order of things. Fight because under these circumstances you must—with neither hatred nor pleasure."

"Fight whom?" Jaybhardan snapped back. "Where is the enemy? The soldiers and chariots, the gruesome weapons, I see them not. I peer into the horizon, yet I see them not. Why did you call me back?"

"Was it I?" Somdev replied, suddenly distant and mysterious.

Jaybhardan stiffened. His father turned his large, familiar mass towards him, eyes boring into his core.

"Indra became invincible by drinking the celestial libation that illuminates the darkness…" he began, in a strange and imposing voice.

"Indra is the god of war!" Jaybhardan interrupted angrily.

"…and the father of medicine," Somdev went on, his pupils glittering. "Indra presided over your birth, attended by Urmila; he will ensure your sovereignty. You will become king of the great human masses. Those drowning in disgrace will be your subjects. Those who are accursed from the womb and worth less than nail parings or donkey urine. Your blessed subjects, reconciled and laved with joy."

His father's face dissolved into many thousand points of colour. Fear took hold of Jaybhardan.

"You want to choose, to protect yourself from the unexpected by refusing everything," his father's remote voice went on. "The void calls to you, you have no experience… Luxury and ease of the counterfeiter! Sunlight makes no distinctions. It shines equally on all beings, peaceable and warlike."

Tears welled in the prince's eyes. The voice went on relentlessly, "I cast out the miserly of heart, the calculating. And I order you: you shall live without sparing yourself."

A heavy silence fell over Jaybhardan; quantities of time flowed towards him from all directions, bearing unnamed masses, lumps, crumbs and transparencies. Shapes abounded in a sea of darkness. The wind finally died down. The landscape ceased its dancing and settled into place around them. The king of Mahisautha was smiling, one hand laid lightly on his son's arm. The latter cried out and threw himself at his father's feet.

"Bhairav Bhoopal," he murmured, flabbergasted. "Shiva's assistant... Lord Shiva, what do you want from me?"

"Will you go?" Somdev asked.

▼

The wind was tearing at the branches as Jaybhardan issued his orders before withdrawing from the scene. When he returned, rows of elephants in armour stood in front of the trees, some of them adorned with gold and rubies, their tusks sanded to sharp points protected by rings. Eagles and kites circled overhead. The horse and elephant tenders checked their supplies of fodder, others made sure the chariots reserved for the commanders of the cavalry and infantry units were in good order.

The soldiers were delighted at having the elephants made available for transporting material and building roads and bridges. Somdev had, however, always imposed certain rules on the chaos of war—neither hatred nor pleasure. Elephants were not to be used to trample the enemy to a bloody pulp—their role must be strictly dissuasive, like mobile ramparts. "Do not stir up memories of when they were captured in the jungle," the king always said. "Don't light a fire around the tranquil mammoths, they are consecrated to exist in a genial and helpful profusion. Of course, there is the terrible upheaval of their mating, but it leads to the birth of stars. Outside of such extreme periods, the elephant is a model of peaceful strength in its relationship with man."

Time passed. Jaybhardan awaited a sign from his father, whose face remained inscrutable. Finally, the wisps of kusha smoke lifted along with the mists floating away from the trees, taking the exhausted mirages and rumours of battle away with them to China.

"You may leave Mahisautha, my son," Somdev commented gently. "As you can see: we have no enemies here."

▼

With his little troop he headed off, climbing onto Bhuranand's back to avoid the clamorous scene, withdrawing into himself with an empty heart. After travelling aimlessly for a while, with no goal in mind, he queried the Elements to know which way to lead the little community that had sprung up around him. The trill of a bird—neither kite nor parrot, nothing either striking or colourful—replied. Immediately, Jaybhardan called out to one of his servants, a young man named Jhinma.

"Follow that bird," he ordered, "and find out where it wants to lead us."

5

Jhinma had no trouble following the most unremarkable bird in the world through the countryside... though he never could have imagined that the bird dwelled on the Mountain in a golden cage, deep within the seven palaces that nestled one inside the other. All around them, nature seemed to be in a state of yearning. Flowers wanted seeds and pods; indigo blossoms swayed their toothy calyces, their sheaves of petals trembling from banner to wing, their red spurs watching for the slightest tremor in the air. The pure and the impure shaded everything in dubious hues from which glowed light nonetheless. Everything was swollen with desire, in the shade and the hot sun, in the thickets and the plains. Now blocking his nostrils, now closing his eyes, Jhinma had to protect himself from temptation.

When the bird reached the lake, it circled over the jasmine-scented Malins, saw on their brows the wedding jewel known as bédouli, snapped it up in its beak and flapped away back to Jaybhardan, with Jhinma chasing after it.

"Heaven and Earth!" the prince exclaimed when he saw it. "What marriage is this? Nothing will ever put it asunder."

Drawn by the light of the jewel, ordinary as it was, Moti Ram, Budeshwar and Karikant came running, their servants on their heels, already thinking about preparing a ceremony in the woods. The prince asked for silence, and was about to withdraw when Bhuranand approached with several of his peers to form a circle around him. Kneeling before its master, the elephant slowly unfurled its trunk to graze Jaybhardan's chest. It was covered in elusive patterns from top to bottom.

"Who painted this sacred geometry on you, Bhuranand?" a disconcerted Jaybhardan asked. "What sign is this?"

Raising its trunk the elephant trumpeted a mighty blast. The trunk pleated itself into thousands of steps disappearing into infinity, then lowered past the ivory gateway of its gigantic tusks drawn like sabres. Dumbfounded, Jaybhardan dismissed everyone but Karikant and his brothers. Perched on Jhinma's shoulders, the bird was still staring at him with its yellow eyes. Jaybhardan reminded himself that he was descended from a royal lineage that included Rama. Like Rama, he too could aspire to ascend to Indra's paradise. He dwelled on Rama, torn between personal interest and the universal, Rama who had detached himself from Sita.

"I cannot accept this jewel, whose loss some young woman must mourn," he declared abruptly. "May it be returned to her immediately."

▼

Dauna and Kushuma were so chagrined at being spurned, they forgot all about the tasks awaiting them at Somdev's palace and slid into melancholy. After a long vacillation, they renounced the idea of returning to Mahisautha and decided that having left everything to follow the prince one day, they would follow him forever.

In this, they were guided from above: "Go to the garden of Pakaria," the wind whispered to them. "He will be there."

"Up until now, he has enjoyed the favours of the palace and his father's wisdom," Krishna pointed out, "but how will he find a way to triumph over love?"

"What do you mean by 'triumph', Krishna? Love is the greatest blessing," said Shiva.

"It stimulates passions that cloud the light," replied Krishna. "It envelops the soul. It overwhelms the mind."

His voice coursed through the breeze, a steady song. His presence could only be discerned by the harmony it engendered everywhere.

"Oh, Krishna, I've heard that speech of yours so often I know it by heart," Shiva exclaimed. 'Be wary of passion!' 'Be wary of covetousness and anger, sister of desire!' 'Voracious One', you say, 'Great Evildoer'. You do repeat yourself endlessly, Krishna."

They had been teasing each other since forever.

"When you disavow those who squander their breath," Shiva went on, "who waver endlessly between vain hopes and vain fears, I approve what you say. But I am talking about Love. About the unblemished fruit and the well-performed action. I'm talking about the undaunted force."

His words resonated everywhere at once.

"...I speak of the opening to the Supreme that brings good to all beings."

He smiled. His three-eyed face spun slowly towards the east. The sun grew larger, foamy with power, and the great healer poured its balm over the Earth. Then he joined Krishna the Blessed One in the sovereign silence, where they shrank together and were conflated into one.

7

Walk, taking the other's pace into consideration. Meditate. In step with the flow, the prince graduated into maturity almost without noticing. They stopped for the day by a pond, not knowing whose land they were on. Jaybhardan immediately asked his young aide-de-camp to set up an altar. Anil stood watching as the prince danced, with the suppleness of a leopard, around the massed offerings of rice, fruit, and incense. He was overcome with tender regard for this heir without a kingdom, who reigned over none but a few servants, three horses and some elephants. Meanwhile, Moti Ram was setting up a rudimentary camp for the men and animals in the park in Ladaniya, near Pakaria, ruled by a man called Bhim Sain.

Jaybhardan was training his body, thrusting and striking at an imaginary opponent, but he had no enemies and never would. He had been taught to shoot with a bow and arrow, a task where one didn't have to touch the unclean. But face to face, chest to chest, he would meet only brothers and would use no other weapons but those of Shiva, the king of dance: he possessed only the spear of the word, of the mind.

Moti Ram awaited his orders along with Budeshwar, Karikant and the mahouts, who were pleased to see their elephants happily munching on the region's plants, when a peasant came running up, arms waving. Although they didn't understand his dialect, he made it clear that he wanted their animals out. He had seen their sick elephants spitting blood like humans and, what's more, he was going to inform King Bhim Sain that Somdev's troop had invaded their territory. The king would chase them out, they'd see! With that, he hightailed out of there, the cloth wound around his frail pelvis bouncing like a cork.

When Karikant asked them about the elephants' health, the mahouts reassured him that there was nothing wrong with them but indigestion from eating beetroot.

"Still, Jaybhardan must present himself before Bhim Sain as soon as possible," Karikant declared.

"There he is," Budeshwar said.

Indeed, Jaybhardan was approaching on Bhuranand's back, distracted by something. On the pond's surface, he had noticed two lotus flowers that were unlike all the others. The yellow of their hearts was as intense as that of the bédouli he had returned.

▼

Moti Ram accompanied him to the palace of King Bhim Sain, to whom they presented apologies for their belated tribute. The king of Pakaria was the same age as their father, Somdev, and his curiosity was piqued. He accepted the tribute with equanimity, before a certain number of his subjects in the throne room. Commanded to relate the circumstances of his departure from Mahisautha, Jaybhardan described his situation.

"Choosing exile is a serious decision, since we can't

know what fate has in store for us," Bhim Sain commented with a ponderous affability. "What is the meaning of your sacrifice, son of Somdev? Are you pursuing enemies? Are you trying to protect those you love from misfortune?"

"My goal is revolutionary," Jaybhardan replied. "I want to deliver the humble from their squalor."

It sounded startling and insolent, but Bhim Sain held his emotions in check and let nothing show. Moti Ram was anxiously gnawing at the skin inside his cheeks.

"Deliver the humble...," the king muttered with calculated calm. "How interesting. And that would be an expression of divine will, I suppose?"

Jaybhardan remained silent.

"I see. So you have sloughed off the privileges and duties of your caste," Bhim Sain went on, a bit heatedly, "your duties as an heir..."

Hands pressed to his thighs, he went on, enunciating carefully like some storyteller, "In. Order. To. Serve..."

At that he looked slowly around his audience—the dumbstruck ministers, the half-kneeling soldiers whose posture signalled their readiness to pounce—compelling all to bear witness, and concluded, "...the meek, the poor, and the impure."

An enormous grin spread across his face.

"Applause, applause, my friends!" Bhim Sain exclaimed, signalling to everyone to do as he said.

Made uneasy, no one budged. Jaybhardan's gaze bored into the king. Rather than turning away, the older man took his time to examine his young visitor carefully.

Those who worship the gods reach for the gods, he was thinking. Why would this brilliant young man limit the form of his worship to such a narrow perspective? He pretended to query the ceiling, entirely carved with geometrical flowers, and wedged himself deep into his imposing wooden seat.

"The moral law you hold up as superior to tradition—I wonder where it is embodied for you, son of Somdev."

Nonplussed, Jaybhardan wavered. A section of the ceiling lowered itself towards him, a mandala with concentric circles inscribed in a square. Diagonals divided the whole into four parts, each in one of the colours of the social classes in Vedic society. His eyes grew wide. He could see tiny servants and peasants, a dizzying number of the impure. They spun like grains of sand, past the dividing lines. Then the lines paled, and all at once, the colours faded, while the king, disguised as his father, kept glaring at and muttering to him, "I wonder where the moral law is embodied for you..."

Jaybhardan caught his breath at last. The syllable sprouted, pushing its way through his throat. "The Om, my boys," the guru used to say. "You carry the 'O' from your chest to your head. Then you transport the physical sound until you achieve consciousness."

So he focused on Bhim Sain and declared in a powerful voice, "I realize that I am not yet ready for such a task, your majesty. What I mean by that is that I am not yet led by a liberated intelligence. For the moment, I do not know who I am or where I am going. My only action consists in offering my absolute availability to the Lord."

Satisfied with Jaybhardan's words, the king's attitude softened. What a singular character, he mused, with standards one rarely sees. Should he achieve balance within reality, he would touch true grace. Has nature ever produced such a man as this, he asked himself. The prince was staring straight ahead, beyond the barrage of guards, beyond the courtiers.

"It is rarely granted to an individual to ignore the rules of the group, Jaybhardan," Bhim Sain concluded.

He invited his ministers to sit before freshly cut leaves, and had a light meal served while he escorted his guests out. He was struck by an idea and wished to speak to them in private.

"Let's get down to business, Jaybhardan," he said firmly. "You may not stay in Ladaniya with your elephants. Rumour has it that they are unwell."

"Every single one of them is in perfect health, your majesty," Moti Ram—whom the king had not yet addressed—burst out, as though his honour depended on it.

Jaybhardan nodded. Bhim Sain pinched his own earlobe.

"Well, in that case everything's fine," he said. "Besides, those beasts are always healthy when they can graze freely, isn't that so? Captive elephants are contaminated by humans and not the other way around... but try explaining that to the courtiers."

"No one could choose healing herbs better than

they," Moti Ram, who had no truck with irony, added.

Bhim Sain waited an instant, burst out laughing, and turned his back on him, directing his attention back to the elder brother.

"Listen, my boy," he went on, clearly tempted to make friends with the prince. "You're going to visit my daughter, Chandravati; she lives in the garden of Pakaria with her retinue. She too knows of your father's reputation, and will spot your nobility, even though it's... how shall I put it? Atypical. Your elephants will find there all the pasture they need."

The two brothers brought their hands together and bowed their heads. More excitable than he had let on, the capricious Bhim Sain suddenly revealed his hand.

"A young man called Chuharmal already serves Chandravati in her garden," he blurted. "But what difference does that make? I have decided today to appoint you guardian of her garden. So you two will be rivals, and he is your cousin. We shall see what comes to pass. The better one between you shall marry my daughter, and I will make him the heir to my throne."

With that, he curtly ordered his soldiers to show them the way to Pakaria.

▼

Instead of flaring up at the idea of having to fight a relative he had never met for a woman he would refuse as a spouse, Jaybhardan let perplexity house itself in his mind. He allowed Moti Ram to relate their adventure to their companions, and had Karikant repeat it to the scribe, Heeraman, whose task it was to transmit their story to posterity. When he was alone, he prayed ardently to Durga, imploring her for guidance. Should he really go to Pakaria?

The goddess wasted no time in informing him of her will.

"You must go there, my son," she replied.

8

The horizon was billowy in the humid weather, soft on the elephants' backs, shivery on the treetops. When they reached Pakaria, the molten sun was oozing through the branches, waiting to crown the noon. The trees tore the last veils of mist open, and the sun flowed in.

The garden had a brilliant spirit that exuded mystery. Beauty brought union to the minds of all beings, and union was rampant throughout the garden. According to Heeraman, the Invisibles themselves fell to straddling the insects.

Famished for love, the Malins were magically transported to Pakaria to await the prince who would raise this extraordinary place to sheer perfectness in their eyes. What they did not know was that Chandravati had caught a glimpse of him at the bamboo gate that marked the entrance to her domain; that she had heard the sound of his voice and imagined the feel of his palm; that she had conceived a violent passion for him. The Malins didn't notice right away that the garden was altering, due to the will of a woman stabbed by desire. The wind had begun to whip the flowers. Branches wailed under its lash. The sun inflamed the jasmine and dried up the hibiscus. For the first time, plants in that magical garden were dying. Bhim Sain's soldiers stumbled upon squirrels lying in the paths, their bellies offered to birds' beaks. Chandravati's servants found butterflies torn in half.

Like the Malins, Moti Ram and Budeshwar turned a blind eye to the torment at first, preferring to see in the garden only the inexhaustible plenitude that had made it legendary: the beauty of its corollas and clusters, its sumptuousness. Jaybhardan did the same. He had followed Durga's command without a second thought. And he had agreed to be made protector of the garden, at the risk of offending his cousin.

"Robust body; broad neck; flat nose and thin moustache, Chuharmal resembles the warrior Yalambar, the first king of the Kirats," the scribe would later write, sharpening his bamboo stylus every day to record the story of the King of the Mountain. "Robust body; thin, flexible neck; shapely nose and thin moustache, Jaybhardan resembles Arjuna, whose protector Krishna lopped Yalambar's head off in order to bring the Great Battle to an end. Fury and sorrow! It would be better for Jaybhardan to wind back the days of his life and return to the divine night."

▼

Princess Chandravati was enchanted by Reshma's painting; it already covered a large section of the garden wall. Wherever the brush passed, her skill had made the stone and clay vanish. Animals, wild and tame, came pouring in. Birds tried to build their nests in the trees she had drawn, spiders to weave their webs between painted leaves.

Perched near a pistachio tree, her sisters, Dauna and Kushuma, had garbed themselves in red and orange to bloom in the shape of blossoms of the flame of the forest, the marvellous tree associated with Shiva that the peasants called palash. As soon as she became aware of their presence, Reshma gave thanks for having seen her childhood companions once again, left her human shape, and herself became a palash blossom.

Dauna and Kushuma were joyful at seeing her, and they congratulated her on her remarkable work. Kushuma gestured towards a beast half-hidden by ferns. "That lion is alive!" she exclaimed.

Reshma blushed. When her fingers had touched the clay, the animal's muscular body had revived the sensation of being in Chuharmal's arms. Dauna noticed, smiled, and nodded wisely. Kushuma did the same, but sadly. They confessed to having shirked their duties to Somdev out of their love for Jaybhardan, whom they had followed to this place.

"At least your love has led you to detach yourself from everything," Reshma replied, almost envying them. "You have learned the austerity of renunciation instead of the worries and yearning of concupiscence."

"What presumption!" Kushuma protested. "The prince spurns us like soiled straw from a stable... and you applaud our affliction, when you anoint your body with sandalwood paste to revel with your Chuharmal!"

"May the prince be an athlete of the mind if he so desires," Dauna added. "May he give himself over to the divine light, since everything around him murmurs that he is beloved by Shiva and will bring justice and a higher reality to mankind... but don't laugh at us, Reshma, because his faith is greater than ours."

Something disturbed the grass beneath the tree. Birds the size of large hens were starting their courtship display—floricans, bustards recognizable by the feathers on the male's head. As handsome as a peacock in a golden jacket with black lapels, the male shook his crest, lifted one yellow claw and pointed his beak towards the female before he began a series of leaps and jumps with fluttering wings that propelled him three cubits in the air. The dull-hued female watched him, crouching on the ground. The three sisters laughed. Dauna and Kushuma wondered at the female's passive behaviour but said nothing out of regard for Reshma. She was about to get down from the tree to continue with her painting when a swan appeared, silhouetted by the sun, waddling towards them from some distance ahead.

"He comes from the lotus pond at the heart of the garden," Reshma whispered to them. "It's very strange, usually he won't let anyone near him."

"Hamsa..." Dauna murmured in surprise. "Symbol of the divine couple, of Shiva's spirit and energy. What message do you come to deliver?"

The swan bowed to them and disappeared in a blaze of white.

Reshma averted her gaze from her sisters transformed by the grace that had just been granted them. She eluded their embrace and jumped down to the ground. Her composure restored by the vegetation that half-buried her in its lush scents, she reached out to pet the lion she had painted so masterfully. Her gaze drowned in the feline's as she continued at her task without turning to look.

Dauna and Kushuma's breath had joined the celestial one that lifted the garden's flower petals. For now, carnal attraction no longer gripped them. The next day, they didn't need to see the prince to know that he was deep in conversation with Heeraman, near the palash and pistachio trees. His soul and theirs were intertwined.

9

From the moment Chuharmal set foot in her garden, the princess had pampered him. To her soldiers, she praised the ardour of his body, his heart of a lion, trained to release its power intelligently in every blow. She commissioned odes from the palace poets in honour of this man who knocked down wild boars, perhaps even bears, with his bare hands. But the princess was fickle; she set this hero aside the instant Jaybhardan appeared on her land.

Fear settled over the prince's entourage at once.

"Chuharmal can't conceive of a rival devoid of arrogance. He's going to want to take revenge on whoever he thinks has usurped his place," Moti Ram commented. "Jaybhardan obeys Durga, and the goddess wears Shiva's anger... That's all very well on the cosmic scale, but what in the here and now? How will a good man's anger find expression?"

"'Remember me and do battle.' Isn't that the divine injunction?" Budeshwar interjected. "What kind of battle will it be?"

"Jaybhardan is aiming to achieve the absolute," Karikant pointed out. "In other words, perfect liberation... But he still needs to abandon both subjectivity and illusion."

"Can detachment help him against Chuharmal? What if humiliation inflames Chuharmal to break Jaybhardan's back in revenge?" Moti Ram snapped back in a bitter voice. "My elder brother is a knottier puzzle than the other. His ideas and acts are not of this world—you'd think he deliberately defends everything we find repellent. Insisting that men and women are equally worthy! And why must he dawdle amongst the impure as though he enjoyed it? Would he have us dwell in filth? May the gods have mercy! Why does he care so much about emancipating the impure, among whom so many crooks and good-for-nothings are to be found? Sometimes, when I think back to that embryo business, it makes me sick."

It got to the point where they wanted to return to the piety of their ancestors. Jaybhardan caught them in conversation with a priest from Pakaria: they wanted to sacrifice a billy goat. As if ending a life could make amends for anyone or anything at all.

"What's this?" he exclaimed. "Killing doesn't bother you? How do you suppose the goat feels about it?"

His smile made their blood run cold. First women, and now billy goats... Plus keeping company with the ugly and deformed, whose meals he agreed to share. Jaybhardan's visage seemed to gain radiance while his brothers found themselves drowning in incomprehension. His was an implacable self-assurance, a grandeur that was not nourished by the least personal ambition. That was the worst part—his appalling innocence. His unbearable, overwhelming innocence.

Believing themselves replaced in the prince's affections by Heeraman and young Anil, the brothers sought out the company of the mahouts. Sitting by the elephants whose ears threw black butterfly shadows on the ground, they spent hours going over and over their favourite topic: Princess Chandravati. Her bewitching beauty seemed not to have the slightest effect on Jaybhardan.

Still, they took him aside more than once and questioned him ruthlessly. Why did he have to stick out by insisting on uniting the pure and the impure? Why act like everything was harmonious and equal, when anyone with eyes could see the opposite was true?

"I have faith in a general intuition," Jaybhardan replied gently.

Sometimes, out of affection for them, he would point a finger to the sky and add, "Perhaps you will also experience the fleeting touch of celestial peace. You never know."

"You never know." That was the last straw for Moti Ram, the absolute limit for Budeshwar. Before Jaybhardan came along, everyone knew what was what! Everyone had their place, and everyone was in it. However lowly or despicable the place, it was preordained, ineluctable. It spared the imagination by flattening out individual wills. It ensured that the palace reigned smoothly, unchallenged, that royal edicts flowed over the populace like melted ghee.

Karikant listened to them getting worked up over the possibility of a rivalry between Jaybhardan and Chuharmal. As though they would be engaged in a battle between good and evil, as though that was their objective. Yet they had all been taught to free themselves from the shackles of action. Without meeting Chuharmal, they had already clothed him in the garb of an enemy. But, for Karikant, spirit generated matter rather than the other way around. And since all existence was soaked in it, Chuharmal had to contain a tiny drop of the Infinite Consciousness, just as they did.

Karikant had no doubt about it, but how could he convince his uncles? And would it change anything? "We shouldn't jump to conclusions about other people," was all he said one night, before walking away whistling.

The minute his back was turned, they went back to their favourite topic.

"Did you see Princess Chandravati, today?" Moti Ram asked softly, mindful of the spies Bhim Sain had surely planted throughout the woods.

"She left for the eastern part of the garden in her palanquin, sheltered behind drawn curtains," Budeshwar whispered back. "I saw her because I was testing the strength of a wall on that side."

"Did you kill many snakes today?" Moti Ram went on.

"Hundreds," boasted Budeshwar, "and spiders as big as Bhuranand's head, but don't tell Jaybhardan."

"Not a word," promised Moti Ram.

Rather than confessing their feelings for the princess, they ascribed them to Chuharmal in the theatre of love they were inventing.

"Chandravati is too fickle," Moti Ram pretended to complain, trying to temper his brother's ardour. "She never should have sent Chuharmal away."

"What do you mean?" Budeshwar was offended. "The princess wants the best guardian for her garden. Is that a crime? Allow me to retire. I need to inspect the buttresses of the western wall, see if they are a sturdy protection for the inhabitants."

"I'm as concerned about them as you are," Moti Ram said, jumping up. "And we both know that the princess's bedroom faces that way. I'm coming with you."

His brothers may have disapproved of his indifference, but Jaybhardan had to apply constant self-control to achieve it; his goal was to feel exactly the same towards everything. He was training himself in the art of concentration so as to maintain it even in his dreams. He sometimes spoke of his projects to Heeraman, described how Somdev had allowed him to map out a new kind of justice in Mahisautha. It required practice to be spread far and wide. He would undoubtedly be attacked, perhaps by his cousin, Chuharmal. But he would prepare for the possibility of blows ahead by meditating, not by polishing weapons.

Heeraman sometimes asked questions to test him. Once it was to determine how he felt about the philosopher Nagarjuna, born under a tree, like him, and who, it was said, had cured Mucilinda, the king of the Nagas. Nagarjuna had followed in the Buddha's footsteps.

"The snakes are our teachers, too," was all Jaybhardan said in reply. "May we observe all that exists without discriminating."

Another time, it had been about disciples of the Tantric path, who seemed rather morbid.

"What bothers you about them, Heeraman?"

The scribe mentioned Shiva's dark blue, southwest-facing head, the one that was named 'fearless'.

"Doesn't it represent profound wisdom? Shiva's gaze

over the universe detached from dualities?" Jaybhardan reminded him. "He doesn't distinguish between the essence of the pure and the impure."

"I've heard those people wear black," Heeraman replied awkwardly, "that when they beg, they hold out a skull in place of a beggar's bowl. People say they feast in crematoriums, on excrement, alcohol and drugs."

Jaybhardan reflected for a moment. Putting a reassuring hand on the scribe's shoulder, he calmly declared, "However we may feel about their customs... the fact is that some minds are open to the ambiguity of reality. Let us not fear anything either. We must love everything."

It seemed to him that his companion was trembling. He brought the tips of his long fingers together and stared at him pensively. "We must not let ourselves be distracted by the outside world, Heeraman," he murmured. "Let us not install each other as obstacles on the divine path."

▼

After the conversation, Jaybhardan retired to the hut assigned to him near the palace. It was almost night, but his brothers were not waiting there, as was customary. They must have eaten earlier with the mahouts, he assumed. He rebuked himself for neglecting Bhuranand, decided to inspect the garden with him the next morning. Stepping inside the hut, he paid no attention to the twin flowers that had sprung up at the foot of a wooden column, one among several holding up the roof of the porch. Listening carefully, he heard Dauna and Kushuma's songs of praise, thanking the heavens for having freed them from carnal desire. He prepared a lightly spiced drink for himself and dozed off on his bamboo mat while thinking of Durga, her feline mount, and her necklace of skulls. The shadows deepened around him, and the darkest night fell.

He was fast asleep when the goddess appeared between the columns of his hut. The porch was covered in paintings that showed her in triumph, the demons Chanda and Munda slain at her feet. Maithils bustled around her, putting finishing touches to her image, in which she was garbed in elephant skin. Others were hastily finishing the mane of her lion, Manashthala. Two young women were painting the thick black outline of her piercing eyes when Chandravati entered, silhouette rippling in the soft light, her body glistening before the dumbstruck dreamer.

"Your reputation precedes you, son of Somdev," Chandravati's painted lips whispered. "My heart has yearned for you these many moons, and I prayed to the gods that my splendour be united with yours. My father will arrange for us to be wed, and Durga will be pleased."

"Durga has many forms!" Jaybhardan countered, without realizing what he was doing. "Leave me in peace, immodest woman! I may be one of those lowly Dusadh you call crooks, but I don't care for your manners."

The spurned princess's fury filled the room, making the paintings on the porch glow red. Jaybhardan barely had time to see the demons rise up on their hind legs, the scales on their thighs clattering as they ran into the night, whimpering. Wanting to wipe the sweat dripping copiously from his brow, he saw that his body was deliquescing.

"Durga, Ganga?" he cried out. "What do you want from me, great goddess? Must I betray myself? Do not tempt me with trinkets."

He leapt from his bed and slipped quietly from his hut to join Bhuranand in his stable. The elephant wrapped its trunk around him, lifted him on to its back and together they strode through the rustling shapes appearing and disappearing in the garden as they ploughed ahead: at first sumptuous and bountiful, the forms gradually became sporadic, murky and opaque.

"Lord!" Jaybhardan implored. "Put false images away from my eyes and evil gossip from my ears. I believe in your Word and beg for guidance."

Bhuranand was making steady progress, his master's hands on the double crown of his head. The great beast led Jaybhardan to the spot where the wall vanished into vegetation.

Jaybhardan slid down the animal's trunk and fell to his knees. Could it be true? Was there no longer a difference between the inside and outside for him?

"You have not yet left ignorance and the weight of the world behind," the wind whispered. "But see, and perceive! Already your soul rises beyond incarnation, liberating itself from its subjection."

He could hear squirrels frolicking far, far away, in the branches of deodars on the side of the Mountain. How could it be? It lasted but an instant, then nothing. Confused, he led Bhuranand back to the stable and returned to his hut.

Lying in ambush behind the hut, Bhim Sain's soldiers pounced on him, laughing and cracking bawdy jokes. One of them struck a hard blow to his head, and he collapsed to the ground. They tied him up and threw him in a dungeon.

11

Lightning streaked the sky over the valley.

"Salhesh doesn't need a wife in the orderly space of ritual," Shiva said. "He will teach justice by unfurling love."

"Let's see it in his actions," Krishna replied with a grin. "Hostility is growing. I hear the growling of wild beasts around him, and crows flap their wings amongst your bolts of lightning. If it comes to counting the dead between Chuharmal and Salhesh... Whatever happens, Chuharmal will be endowed with sons, not Salhesh. No sons, no rites. And without rites, no salvation."

"Why summon mourners?" Shiva thundered. "To trace a line in the sand that demons may not cross? Besides, what demons? Listen, Krishna: there is no dividing line. Salhesh is reaching for the immeasurable. If he learned archery from Arjuna, it was to shatter the horizon."

"Granted... Let us celebrate together," Krishna replied. "I have repainted the double curve of his eyebrows so that everyone can read in them the sacred syllable—the seed of all knowledge and the sign of unity.

"Bravo, Krishna," Shiva riposted. "Still, lean over this way a bit."

Vapour was rising from the hot earth, and mist was nestling in barely opened corollas. Shiva pointed down at Dauna and Kushuma.

"What do you see?" he asked.

"Two magicians, flower-women," Krishna replied. "I see in them love and matter, the earth and transmission via the rites."

"First love, which will overflow separations and measurements, and dissipate mortal constraints," Shiva said.

Dauna and Kushuma were keeping an eye on Chuharmal. They had perceived his hatred and understood his sway over their little sister. Not one square inch of the man's beloved body was unknown to her, but she did not realize that the ambition burning in his heart prevented him from having the slightest esteem for her.

"Ganga," Chuharmal prayed, standing before the river, "Mokama reeks of strong spices, and the screeching of the birds exhorts me to do battle. You who were born in the Himalayas, look at me, and judge what I am made of. Which tree am I most like: the deodar, the juniper, the oak of the plains? Am I not more than a hazelnut tree? See this woman at my feet? Every day, I draw life-force from her, but I need more."

"How vehement he is!" deplored the sisters hidden in the purple blossoms of a nearby tree. "Such loathsome pride."

"I was the guardian of the garden, Ganga," Chuharmal went on. "Give me back my rightful place in Chandravati's palace, and then grant another request, I beg of you: I must drink from the princess's vase and slake myself with the bracing juices of a higher rank."

"Pretentious! Ridiculous!" the sisters thought. "Where is his virtue?"

"Grant me that woman," he repeated adamantly, "and I will be your devotee forever. They say she lies on a bed of gold that makes lovers godlike."

Chuharmal beseeched the goddess with such insolence that in the end the heavens came down against him.

"Unworthy man!" the wind breathed. "To reach the woman you covet, you will crawl below ground. You will approach her, but will touch her not. You will be able to take only what she is not—her jewels, her dazzling gown, and the fabulous bed that grants godlike pleasure. You will steal the bed, and another will be accused of the crime, but you will get no pleasure from it."

"He is blind and deaf to what matters most," the sisters buzzed, tucked within the branches of the purple tree. "He will crawl like a mole, with shovels for hands. He will steal the wondrous bed, but he will never know the ardour of Shiva embracing Parvati."

Haunted by desire and spurred on by Ganga to indulge the excesses of his nature, Chuharmal became obsessed with the idea of digging a tunnel through the garden to break into the palace. He rushed through his prayers, convinced himself that the tunnel was his own idea, congratulated himself for being so clever, and rushed headlong towards his fate.

He insisted on digging and persisted in crawling. The goddess Ganga howled with laughter to see him—filled with male sap, boiling with jealousy against his cousin, the son of Somdev. She submerged him in passion, lifted him up and tossed him towards Chandravati, and he dug and scratched and crawled, tossing shovelfuls of earth with furious growls. Underground, he escaped the attention of the soldiers, guards, horses and elephants. Swollen with power and eager to fight the king of the Nagas—whose home he destroyed without a care—he meant to burst, bedecked in new glory, into the princess's chambers and overpower her, serpents draped like necklaces on his chest, twining around his wrists like bracelets.

He had even convinced Reshma to assist him in wreaking his revenge. Her role would be to coax the princess along by describing the throes of divine passion, before pouring a potion into her beverage that would send her into a deep sleep. The sensual carvings set into the wood of the wondrous bed would fire her imagination, the drug-induced fever would do the rest: Chandravati would fall into a delirium.

Reshma obeyed his odious command, and everything went as Chuharmal had planned. When night came, Chandravati fell into a divinely scented sleep. The fibres of the wooden bed dripped pure gold, drenched in the luminous fluids of celestial lovers.

Caked in mud, he burst into her room and flew, radiating virile energy, towards her; but for naught, prevented by the divine injunction: You will approach her, but will not touch her. He shook himself free of his desire, lifted Chandravati from her bed and laid her gently on the chest where her servant had placed her silk garments. With cold eyes, he stripped her naked, ripped off her corset of pearls, her undergarments embroidered with a silver-and-gold sun, her belt of tiny gems set in twists of silk, and dove back underground, ashamed of his spoils, yet carrying the plundered golden bed on his head. When he came up from his tunnel, leagues away, his neck and back felt shattered, the bed had struck him mercilessly, the embroidery scratched, the jewels bit. He was sick to his stomach, and had abandoned all hope. In Mokama, he buried the treasure near his house, and Reshma helped him. He had felt the force of Ganga pounding in vain through his body, and Chandravati's naked body had scarred him with mortal fear.

Yet he went to complain to the goddess for having made him crawl beneath the earth. She reminded him that he was made of both earth and water. Was he willing and able to dedicate his entire existence to an aspiration to enlightenment? Heavens, no! Far from it. He dizzied himself with macerated hemp, and covered his body in ashes, but aside from that? He drank himself into a stupor regularly, ate both fish and meat, toyed with his male member without restraint and daily plundered Reshma's flesh. And where had it got him? It was time to look inside himself and plumb his own heart! To rip out the bile that filled him, and to start by cleansing himself of envy and jealousy.

When he was completely demolished, Ganga took pity on him.

"Chuharmal, I will continue to help you," she said. "Listen: you will fight with your rival on a bridge on his way towards the Mountain. You will have Water on your side, and he will have Air on his. Perhaps you will win the battle."

He furrowed his brow warily.

"Why, Ganga?" was all he dared to say.

"The lion is your ancestor," the goddess replied, "but elephants are clouds. Everything that gashes, pierces and destroys will be on your side. Try to appeal to Durga's lioness, whom your cousin honours."

Chuharmal's jaw relaxed and he declared, "I will poke holes through the paunches of those pachyderms, and their guts will spill everywhere, slicking the countryside with slime. Livers, spleens, hearts, and lungs... all in one strike. The bridge will be the bow, and I the arrow it shoots to the tip of the Mountain."

Returning home, he got drunk and took his anger out on Reshma. She could see that humiliation had blinded him, and she shrank beneath his blows, unable to name her misery.

Flattened against the western wall, Moti Ram and Budeshwar lurked like criminals. Over the course of this strange night, they had caught glimpses of soldiers dashing across the woods towards Jaybhardan's hut, and had even heard them give someone a good thrashing, but hadn't understood until later that that someone was Jaybhardan himself. Two sneering soldiers had walked by without seeing them, discussing a dungeon they had never heard of before. Had their brother really been imprisoned in the garden? Jaybhardan must have committed a truly horrible deed.

Instead of being cast aside, the idea stirred their blood, and a cloud of anger towards him burst within them. Their admiration for their elder brother soured instantly into disdain, and its keenness cut like a knife.

"I'm telling you that Jaybhardan has violated Chandravati," Moti Ram muttered. "Why else would Bhim Sain's soldiers toss him into a dungeon?"

"All that prudishness was meant to hide his obsession with vice," Budeshwar capped his brother. "Anyone who appears to be without mediocrity is quite simply someone who has perfected dissembling in how he presents himself."

They got so worked up that they raised their voices and were spotted by the soldiers. One on horseback shouted out their position, and twenty more burst out of a copse.

"Why are you skulking near the palace in the dark?" the first soldier challenged them harshly. "The elephant master entered Princess Chandravati's chamber. He stripped her of her jewels and clothes, and stole the golden bed in which she slept. You must be his accomplices! You belong in the dungeon with him!"

▼

They were tossed in head first. Cross-legged on the dirt floor, Jaybhardan was waiting for them. At first all they could see were rats scampering around him, playfully tracing signs in the dirt. Then they saw his face, and his innocence was plain as day. His was the untroubled face of a free man. They wanted to throw themselves at his feet to beseech his forgiveness, but it seemed as though the earth was sucking them irresistibly towards its centre. He held them tight.

"We are torn between attraction and repulsion," he said, simply. "We undoubtedly need to experience the awkward embrace of opposites."

Moti Ram bit his lip. They had betrayed him in their own minds, and he didn't even resent them for it? That was all he had to say?

"Yes, of course" Jaybhardan replied, "that's all there is to say."

Jaybhardan was great, he was very great, but he still didn't know that the heavens had their reasons for binding Dauna and Kushuma to him. After a long, listless silence,

Budeshwar's eyes widened and he spoke witlessly, "A woman outside will help us. I'm sure of it."

Moti Ram was suspicious. "What makes you think that, Budeshwar?"

"I don't know," replied the despondent Budeshwar. "Because we need help."

"A woman's energy can achieve anything," Jaybhardan murmured.

▼

At that precise moment, Dauna and Kushuma were on their way to Bhim Sain's palace, brooding on the dungeon he had built but never used before. It was so well hidden in the middle of the garden that life in Pakaria went on as though it weren't there, with humans and animals living in harmony. Resources were so abundant that even the arrival of a herd of elephants had been no trouble. The people of Pakaria could have forgotten all about the dungeon, but it fascinated them like the death lurking within their flesh. Its presence was a dark, negative pole that gripped Bhim Sain, too.

The cell was smaller than a hermit's; its geometry eluded measurement because of the loose, unstable soil on which it stood. To keep from getting sucked into it like in quicksand, Moti Ram and Budeshwar had to curl up against Jaybhardan, who remained calm and stable. Four builders had worked on digging it, and all four had perished, swallowed by the mire. Bhim Sain couldn't remember if that was hours or years ago. Time melted away around the hungry prison. Before it, fear had not existed in the garden. The fear came no doubt from afar, growing more intense closer to the dungeon, where suddenly, the past, one's senses and reason were all swallowed up. That's why the people of Pakaria called it 'The Path-Eater'.

Bhim Sain wondered if the jail could devour even fear itself, making way for an empty exaltation like that brought on by chronic poverty. Although the Lord had not moved into his heart to provide the response he yearned for, Bhim Sain had yielded to his love of risk by digging a dungeon that linked to death. Now he had to live with the sorrow of seeing it everywhere: huge beneath the skirts of the flowers, the cornucopia of leaves and fruit. Fear became his constant companion, and his soldiers' as well.

They informed him that the prince was meditating at the centre of the accursed place that seemed to have no effect on him. Perhaps Jaybhardan wasn't really from Mahisautha. Perhaps he was a wandering relative of the wild geese whose flight formation suggested a quest for the absolute.

In order to obtain an audience with the king, Dauna and Kushuma pointed out that they were the descendants of Mahesh Bhandari, who had once reigned over Taregnagadh. They had received an excellent education from their people, could paint marvellously well, and knew the secrets of medicinal plants to appease the ailments of both body and soul. Bhim Sain agreed to receive them, and regretted it at once.

"Honourable Bhim Sain, release Jaybhardan," the Malins pleaded. "He covets neither your daughter Chandravati nor your possessions. The only thing the prince enjoys in this world is that most sacred of foodstuffs, brahmaudana rice, which is almost without a form or substance. He will leave your garden to go to the Mountain, where he will reign just and true: in his eyes, the Lord is everywhere equally, in a temple as in a pit. His heart is so large that nothing is excluded from it."

Their words irked Bhim Sain.

"You have three days to prove his innocence," he told them curtly. "On the fourth, his head will fly."

"We will find the guilty party and bring him to you," the sisters swore.

Far from satisfying him, their audience only increased the king's anxiety, because Jaybhardan's value clearly outshone his own, as though the prince had already been freed from the cycle of birth and death. Bhim Sain would have enjoyed following his heart's instinct. But he could understand neither why he had loved Jaybhardan from the moment he set eyes on him, nor why he would not allow himself to give in to that sentiment.

Sitting in the pit, Jaybhardan rose up like a bird. Shiva saw his spirit soaring and wheeling around Mount Kailash, where he was at rest, and pointed it out to Krishna: "Isn't it the presence of my servant Jaybhardan that I feel nearby?"

"It is he," *Krishna replied with a grin.*

"He shall take the name of Salhesh from this moment on, and all living souls shall acknowledge him as the King of the Mountain!" *Shiva proclaimed.* "He will not be unworthy."

"May it come to pass as you say," *Krishna assented.*

15

The prison opened. The three brothers came up, dazzled by the grace of the women who had freed them. Heeraman omitted to describe their adventures together on the road to Mokama under the watchful eyes of the goddesses Durga and Ganga. All he recorded was that Dauna and Kushuma blended into a single flesh-and-blood woman, who spoke thus to Salhesh: "You and I will disguise ourselves as a couple of Natins, those nomads who offer tattoos as a way to get into people's homes. We shall fill a cart with trinkets and knock on Chuharmal's door. If he's in a good mood, he will want to buy some cheap jewellery for our sister, Reshma. I will dance seductively and draw him to his bed. On his knees before me, he will confess his evil deeds, and tell me where he has hidden the spoils. Then you can capture him and we will take him as our prisoner to Bhim Sain's palace."

But Salhesh disapproved of the ruse. Dauna and Kushuma understood that they would have to go ahead without him and use spells to erase the whole episode from his mind after. So it ensued that with the gods' approval, he and the two-women-in-a-single-body walked to Mokama disguised as Natins, loaded up with inkpots, bamboo writing instruments, and trinkets for sale.

"We are looking for a kind-hearted man named Chuharmal," the two Malins in a single body said, spinning their skirt and swaying their head, which was crowned with orange-hued blossoms of kusum.

"Do you see the wattle-and-daub hovel over there?" was the reply. "That's where you'll find him."

Nimble-footed, they strode towards it, the Two-Women-in-One cheerful, Salhesh looking severe, as if he had swallowed pungent herbs. Not far off, they could hear dogs barking. Chuharmal appeared in the doorway, his brow creased. He didn't notice Salhesh, whose face Durga had clouded so that Chuharmal wouldn't recognize his rival's beauty. Chuharmal looked down on the Nats: he ignored the man, but when he saw the woman haloed in saffron-yellow, hips wiggling and bracelets tinkling, he thought he recognized the goddess Matangi, guardian of one of those subtle paths to knowledge inaccessible to ordinary mortals. Matangi's skin was green; she was the goddess of the Untouchables because she was free of the distinction between pure and impure.

"Ah! It would delight me to know you!" Chuharmal exclaimed, bewitched by the swaying body and the strange hue of her skin.

He snapped at Reshma to leave, and led the woman within, telling the man he should stay outside and keep an eye on their merchandise. He fell headlong into the trap that had been set for him.

The kusum-crowned creature immediately offered her host a tattoo. All he need do was to lie down on his mat.

"What image shall I imprint on your skin, worthy

man?" she asked, as he undressed.

"Hanuman," he replied in a strangled voice. "I want to be inhabited by the god."

"Hanuman," she echoed seductively, touching the muscles of his chest. "He will make of you a formidable warrior. Like the god, you will fly over obstacles... And you will overcome your enemy, who will offer virtually no resistance."

Her fingers pressed his thighs gently.

"Where on your body shall we draw Hanuman, Chuharmal?" she asked in her sweetest voice. Hardly breathing, he touched his chest.

"Oh no," the sly woman protested. "Hanuman will need your whole back for a canvas."

Then with a light touch, she stroked his thigh. Weakened by vanity, he turned over, exposing his back; the Two-Women-in-One began outlining the strong-jawed god's face. His nose was human, as were his eyes and his smile.

"Don't move," said the false Natin, jabbing with her needle over and over, while glancing at the door that was opening slowly. Hanuman's crown and the jewels he wore around his chest would present no particular difficulty.

When Salhesh jumped on Chuharmal to pin him down, the top-right quarter of the wrestler's back was already covered with the monkey god's face. Salhesh barely had time to realize it, but from beneath the long, midnight-blue eyebrow the eye saw him. The Two-

Women-in-One leapt back in fear. Hanuman incarnated loyalty, parents held him up as an example to their children. The god had good reason to condemn their duplicity, so he was granting Chuharmal his energy. Mad with worry, the two Malins in one woman turned to face Salhesh, whose gaze was unblinking.

The next day, they brought their prisoner to King Bhim Sain, along with Chandravati's golden bed and her personal effects. Bhim Sain kept his word: he had the prince, whom he loved, escorted to the boundary of his lands and let him go along with his entourage, their horses and elephants. They headed for the Mountain with no regrets for the garden they were leaving behind, and a thick fog fell behind them.

▼

Princess Chandravati demanded Chuharmal's head, but the gods intervened. The king opened the dungeon his daughter had had him thrown into, and Hanuman bore him through the air to the foot of the Mountain, escorted by celestial messengers. Chuharmal crossed the bridge that the monkey-headed god pointed out to him and waited for Salhesh there.

Having lost her lover, Reshma lost her mind. She continued to paint trees, flowers, and birds on the garden wall, but they wilted, even dragging real ones down with them. The trees of the garden shrivelled up, the birds' crests fell off. The king's subjects deserted

Pakaria. As soon as Reshma finished the wall, it and the garden both crumbled; the dungeon swallowed them up, along with the inconsolable young woman. Thousands of parrots gathered in the air over the place where she disappeared to honour her unrequited love, and legend has it that the garden came back into bloom. According to another legend that Heeraman heard from local peasants, Princess Chandravati sometimes haunted Pakaria in the guise of a pauper who lived among the crows with Alakshmi, the goddess of misery. As for what befell King Bhim Sain, in some good or evil place, Salhesh's scribe noted that one might believe whatever one wished.

Edmund, as soon as Roshina finished, let with it and the garden look troubled; the dungeon shadowed them up along and the face of the young reader. Thereof he gazed steadily... over the place... and here it is not... He gently... took into gloom. No thing in another's gaze that I see... in his... room real pleasure. Jean-Paul Oracle... it is sometimes... P.I.... is... issue of a... prisoner who lived 12 days... grow with... the... of reserve. As he was... Ring Shimbaba... some gentler... delight. Strike it for the more that one might believe whatever one will of.

3

1

Little by little, the sky grew heavy with clouds that settled low over the valleys and the shivering Ganga plain. It tamped the clouds into any available fissures, draped them over the branches of trees, stuffed them into the many mouths of the earth. Directly above sheets, clumps and shreds of land, the sky pumped the clouds like a cow's milk-swollen udder, hosing a soil already saturated with the roiling flow of chagrin. The earth that protested Sita's sacrifice was now mourning Reshma's fate, even as the river stirred the women's tears with the ashes of the dead. Her gleaming waters rivalled the iridescent bellies of the clouds, swollen with the echoes of past tragedies.

For the moment, there was growing tension in the countryside where a bridge of arrows had sprung up on the path towards the Mountain. Throngs of women lined both banks, unmoving, faded by waiting. Silhouettes swayed like plants, each one alone in the midst of a patient crowd, eternally silent and forever dying. Thousands of Sitas, thousands of Reshmas, thronged both sides of the bridge built by Krishna and Shiva; while peasants multiplied offerings and implored the protection of the gods of their villages—the kind of gods that attend to small aspirations and meagre needs. Upstream, dry-lipped sadhus scrutinized the turgid waters at the confluence of the Yamuna, indifferent to human tragedies. But soldiers were polishing their weapons under the trees, muscles rippling as they bent their souls to the iron of their will. War was in the air.

Chuharmal kneeled over the Ganga to query her face. What kind of warrior would he be? He asked the gods for a thousand men like himself, toughened by the discipline of the arena, able to fight with sword or stick. He had Hanuman's strength, now he had to obtain his wisdom. The love of women would lead him astray no longer, but wisdom demanded setting aside one's pride. Righteousness had stood besmirched when the fickle Chandravati humiliated him by preferring the son of Somdev. To quiet his own aching wound and attract Rama's spirit, he needed to steep himself in a commitment to justice alone.

"Listen carefully," he said to his reflection. "Today, I am Rama. I will put all my honour in the service of the law. I am the hero that deserves victory, and Ganga will grant it to me. Who does that prince of Mahisautha think he is? He fled his kingdom and has accomplished nothing to speak of. Who will follow a champion of the poor who isn't even capable of fulfilling the duties of his rank?"

Leaning over the water, he could see all the way down to the muck and mire at the bottom as he continued his dialogue with himself.

"What does that great soul offer the world? To fell hierarchies and replace them with equality between all beings? A uniform mediocrity? What coarse naivety!"

As he spoke he began to grin, exposing large teeth.

His smug conclusion: "They say he's got the people thinking. There are rumours of an unprecedented peaceful revolution. But, for those of us raised to be warriors and knights, there is no value greater than showing your worth in battle."

He had learnt that his adversary would oppose him with elephants, which was unfortunate. He was not prepared for them. They weren't afraid of water; in fact, they swam like fish.

Still, he stood up full of vigour and summoned the companions of his youth: Mohendra, Birendra and Karakulak the Jackal.

"Sacrifice is essential to keep the Cosmic Wheel turning," he declared, inspecting them. "Tell me, what are we going to offer the divine Ganga?"

"A horse?" ventured Mohendra, to flatter him.

Birendra just shrugged. "That would take a year of preparation and would be pointless. We have neither king nor queen." Chuharmal glared at him, but Karakulak the Jackal hadn't weighed in yet.

"With the gods, sincerity is what counts," he said. "We shouldn't put on airs. I'd offer up a goat."

The brief conversation opened a breach that let doubt slip into their leader's mind. The straight and narrow was a surprisingly difficult path. Chuharmal's sacrifice was being offered in exchange for personal advantage— precisely what tarnished a sacrifice. Yet he had never before gathered his ideas into such a magnificent, powerful and noble intention. "His sacrifice..." The words reverberated in his heart like the sounding of Krishna's divine conch shell before battle.

Chuharmal dismissed his companions and went back to the river. A moment later, garbed in nothing but his dhoti, he dove into the icy water. Reassured, pleased with the strength of his well-trained body, he climbed back out of the water, and spread his cloth to dry on the riverbank. The thought came to him that he would need seven hundred well-sharpened daggers to slay his rival's elephants—Ganga had shown images of both the course of action and the result: a greyish muddle. "It's that easy!" he gloated. "Ganga has granted me inspiration." Nonetheless, he felt faint at the sight of his dhoti—adamantly white and seemingly detached from its surroundings. He lay there for a little while, naked and unable to move, then for a while longer, until stupid words enlivened his tongue: "O soul of mine! Are you spotless?"

His men must have finished preparing for combat. The priest would be waiting for him. He regained his composure, convinced that someone had cast a spell on him. At that precise instant, Ganga showed him her waters, on which the hues of sunset had been laid. He saw the twilight colouring his dhoti too, and leapt up in relief to wrap it around himself. Commanding his companions a moment later, his face glowed with the signs of a relentless courage that would ensure their victory.

▼

As for Salhesh, he had been listening to nature, with Heeraman and Anil by his side. A battle was coming? Karikant and his brothers would do whatever was needed, but he hadn't the slightest idea what that might be. "The spirit doesn't yield to violence," he was in the habit of saying. "In the face of adversity, we must dig deeper into the single consciousness that animates all bodies, irrespective of modes of existence... The same consciousness in the goat and the hand that immolates it, in friend and foe."

The same one also in Chuharmal and him.

"Granted, Salhesh," Heeraman said, "but the world imposes its rules. You must see things as they are: Chuharmal feels wronged, and the offence burns within him."

See things as they are? The world imposes its rules? What did Salhesh ever think about but reality? The Great Reality. And the rights of every being, starting with the oppressed, whom he wished to save from the powerful and their shows of pride. He went on, with flagrant joy, "Bodies will dissolve soon, my friend, to expand into the whole universe. Chuharmal's, mine... and those of all the men and woman waiting for a senseless battle on either side of a bridge."

Anil looked at Heeraman in despair. Struggling to contain the sorrow bursting in his chest, he withdrew, horrified. They would soon step on to the bridge of arrows. Salhesh was still claiming that there was no distinction between himself and that beast Chuharmal;

spinning his lovely nonsense, he would lead them straight into a massacre.

Heeraman knew perfectly well that the troops led by Moti Ram and Budeshwar were hardly battle-ready. The goddess Durga had granted Salhesh just seven hundred elephants and seven hundred men who weren't even soldiers. They were peasants and merchants, barbers, pandits and fishermen; Brahmins who came accompanied by their gardeners; and young men between two births, who, on the eve of receiving the sacred thread, had renounced the introduction into their caste. Men of all ages and conditions had flocked to them with their five garments; and musicians drawn from neighbouring lands by the power of his words. Salhesh had maintained the habit of letting them regroup each day at the same time, under a banyan tree, where it was Anil's privilege to introduce him.

Having learned long ago to honour simplicity as a virtue, Salhesh wore neither a headpiece nor an embroidered cape to indicate his status, he flaunted neither a heron feather nor a sword. Of late, a sparse beard had come to trace the outlines of his jaw, and his followers had rushed to mirror him: a light beard and a well-trimmed moustache and long hair rolled into a topknot had become a kind of uniform for the troops his brothers were now reviewing. At first, he had been pleased, believing that his companions were promoting egalitarianism, and that they wished for it as ardently as he. But his feelings soon changed.

Chuharmal's emissaries came to inform him, with shows of pomp and circumstance, that their attack would take place two days hence. This on the advice of the astrologers their leader had consulted. It would be useless for Salhesh to seek a consultation with other astrologers, useless even for him to give battle, as the Heavens had decided in Chuharmal's favour.

Salhesh hadn't the slightest intention of doing so, nor of explaining why not. All the less in that he hadn't the slightest idea about how to triumph through anything other than courage and honour, the foundation of his confidence in human nature. He sent the emissaries back with a heavy heart and a confused mind; counting on divine inspiration, he still climbed to his rostrum to address the throng of his followers.

The tree that sheltered the rostrum stretched its branches and roots perfectly between the earth and the heavens. Salhesh, in a trance-like state, expressed his gratitude towards this natural lute. One day, the Himalayan cedar's branches would filter the sounds of the world, offering him a foretaste of the tonality of the absolute. The gospel he would spread from the Mountaintop would flow, invigorating and consistent, down every slope and flank. So long as the message came from the very top, the precise peak.

Near him, Moti Ram cleared his throat, and Salhesh realized that his trance was a nightmare of self-aggrandizement. The Himalayas as a pyramid, with him at the top, above everyone else! When all creation was bathed equally in divine energy! When the divine permeated every being to its marrow! He was staggered. All around the rostrum, the crowd waited expectantly for him to open his mouth. He opened his eyes instead. When he saw the men with their sparse beards and their topknots facing him, resembling him, he shook with fear. No, this was no way to express equality; no, have mercy, no! What could this mean? Was he grown so enamoured of himself that they assumed he would wish to see his own image everywhere he looked? Did he have so little consideration for his friends that they should wipe off their own faces and deny their individuality to please him? Horror could be read on his face. Durga swooped down to slay his demons, and he burst out in anger at himself. To let himself be seduced by the idea of sitting on the Mountaintop! He went from bright red to pale in an instant.

"Where are the women?" he asked in a quivering voice.

Moti Ram and Budeshwar hadn't heard him.

"The women," Salhesh repeated, in a harsher voice. "Why are we hiding them away?"

Someone shrugged with incomprehension, and pointed to the mass of skirts and saris colouring the riverbank. Salhesh went on, "Stuck in the ground like bamboo, waiting for a massacre that will deprive them of their husbands and sons? Tucked away in the background? But there is no 'background' any more, do you hear me? No top or bottom. The women come with us. We are nothing without them. Go fetch them."

The men stared at each other incredulously, and Salhesh's transfigured silence fell over their shoulders. For a moment, he appeared before them in the glory of Shiva the Benefactor come to destroy ignorance and evil. Young Anil tried to see if his master had three eyes; he wasn't carrying a trident or garbed in a tiger skin, just the white loincloth that covers men's bodies from their navels to mid-thigh. That part of Salhesh was missing, or it was dazzlingly white.

"The Ancients teach that love is the bride of duty," Salhesh spoke softly. "Duty is expressed in not harming others. We need to understand this."

Several men in the crowd shrugged.

"Women should love their husbands," someone shouted, "and the husbands do battle. That's the natural order of things."

"Women for life and men for death? Things aren't that cut and dried," Salhesh replied. "Do you think respect for life is a passive virtue? It requires strength and courage. Consciousness. You shake your heads, but it's true. Consciousness. Have I not spoken to you enough about the power of consciousness?"

Karikant smiled. Heeraman too. Anil stared at his hero's face even harder, and his heart blossomed. Salhesh went on, imperturbable.

"Duty is just a concept. But energy, action—the power of transformation is the power of love."

Dismay ran through the crowd. A young carpet merchant challenged him, his jaw jutting out. "What kind of nonsense is that? Women are supposed to go into battle now?"

"Men defend ideas, not life," Salhesh replied. "They trample it every day—and I'm not even talking about wartime. They do it in their decisions and attitudes, without even realizing it. That's why we need the women with us in all circumstances. Here and now, meaning on this bridge we want to cross."

Karikant blinked.

Moti Ram and Budeshwar grew worried: "What should we do?"

"Let every man go fetch his wife, his sister, his mother, or a neighbourhood woman," Salhesh declared to the men staring at him.

2

They withdrew, and he closed his eyes and dove back into silence.

A strange night fell over the countryside. It covered the bridge and the riverbanks, and swallowed up Chuharmal's soldiers. From a distance, nothing could be seen but his bronze breastplate studded with jewels, and Salhesh's immaculate loincloth, like a kind of cross suspended in the air. Then night devoured them as well. When there was nothing left of them but the drumming of their hearts, Salhesh saw Shiva's trishul glowing in the dark. A woman sat on each of its prongs, tender and beautiful, with the features of Dauna, Kushuma and Reshma. They gleamed resplendent for a moment, before the Mountain appeared in a glimmering bluish haze that spread across the entire firmament.

Had he dozed off? He was surrounded by men, their wives at their sides. He sighed and invited them to sit with him. Finally, he unclenched his shoulders and his words spread over them, peaceful and vast like a slack sea. He entrusted all gathered to the divine will, along with Bhuranand and his seven hundred elephants. His confident eyes swept over them now as happily as if he were contemplating a basket of flowers.

Anil must have slipped from meditation to boredom. Outer noises were prickling his ears. Suddenly he sounded the alert, "King Salhesh!" he cried. "It is time:

Chuharmal's attack has begun."

True, they could hear the chants of the approaching warriors. The commotion was instantaneous amongst the peasants and merchants who were already regretting having sided with a prophet. No sacrifice had been offered to Durga. How could they fight without her on their side? Why had no altar been raised?

The musicians struck up a chant that was meant to call out to the goddess's feline mount.

"Let us straighten our alignments, my friends," Salhesh, still feeling open, said with inopportune radiance.

In truth, he hadn't made up his mind about anything yet.

From the seething crowd on the verge of insurrection, a brave woman in a flower-covered skirt burst into his field of vision. She was leading her cow on a rope and mumbling excuses. Her husband had gone to fetch her, and she was late because she'd had to feed her animals. Salhesh leapt up and reached his arms out to her.

"Welcome, dear sister," he said, looking straight at the cow. "You have arrived at the perfect time."

The crowd swayed with angry people pushing this way and that. He paid them no attention. Little by little, the noise and movement faded away.

"Surabhi, cow of abundance, mother of Shiva's breath, here you are," he murmured in gratitude, speaking to the animal. "I looked at you, and you recognized me. We need no other rites. You will lead us to liberation."

When he opened his eyes for good, he was alone with her, a rope around her neck. Everyone had jumped into the Ganga, and Chuharmal was crossing the bridge with ten horsemen. His horse's powerful hooves squeaked in their iron cladding as it reared up before Salhesh, whose face was glowing gently.

3

"Here they are, face to face," Shiva commented.

"I recognize that bridge," Krishna said. "Or at least, it reminds me of another one."

Shiva smiled.

"Hanuman's challenge to your protégé, Arjuna. You know very well that humans connect me to Hanuman... I know your story: Arjuna wondered why the great Rama would call on the monkey-headed god rather than building a bridge of arrows to free Sita, imprisoned in Lanka. Offended, Hanuman challenged Arjuna to build one like it without any help."

"A childish quarrel!" Krishna replied. "Arjuna was sufficiently aware of Hanuman's power, for he did unfurl a banner with Hanuman's effigy in the plain of Kuru soon after."

"Kurukshetra, the place of the Great Battle between darkness and light. So look down there: all potentialities can be seen at the foot of the bridge that leads to the Mountain."

The wind blew the clouds before them. The air and the water swirled, and the Himalayas shifted imperceptibly on their celestial wheels, the better to receive the sun.

"We have gone beyond chivalrous ideals," Shiva added. "Salhesh seeks to reveal something greater."

"I can't wait to see what your prophet-king can do in terms of magic," Krishna replied.

"Precisely! Let's talk about that secret weapon Arjuna passed on to his son Abhimanyu when he was still in the womb. The secret of the magic circle."

"Don't muddle me with that embryo business!" Krishna exclaimed. "Arjuna couldn't pass the whole secret to his son's embryo because the mother fell asleep halfway through... And when the son, who grew up to become as great a warrior as his father, fell into a trap, Arjuna could do nothing to save him: he was nowhere nearby. Salhesh is hanging back from the battle, too. Did he go to war to defend Somdev's kingdom? Does he wish to fight Chuharmal?"

"Hanging back out of lucidity, not blindness," Shiva replied. "Admit it, Krishna. Salhesh fights only the ignorance that lays the groundwork for violence."

"I admit it," Krishna granted, as his blue skin darkened to night, like a promise of new stars.

4

Salhesh's eyes bored straight into Chuharmal's, and he felt perfectly at home in the clear water of his cousin's gaze. His thoughts dissolved into it along with his cares, the chains of logic and of illusory conquests to come. There was no longer any distance between his cousin and himself: neither fear nor pleasure or displeasure, nothing to take or banish. Nonetheless, Chuharmal was armed to the teeth. He saw Salhesh in a state of beatitude, and believed that he wanted to kiss his eyelids.

"Violation!" he roared, waving him away.

On that, he pulled himself together in a fury and turned towards his horsemen to order them to charge at the enemy, leaving Mohendra, Birendra and Karakulak the Jackal stunned, incapable of understanding why their leader, seething with righteous hatred, had suddenly dissolved into tears while shouting for war.

Vultures rushed in from the fissured sky, swooping straight towards the fainting warrior. So Chuharmal pulled himself together and beseeched Ganga. His soldiers threw themselves into the water after Moti Ram's troops and their women, whom they spared. But their daggers sought out the majestic bodies of the elephants, stabbing at them ruthlessly in the heaving waters, and the monsters were expelled from the mire by the impact of the attack. Metal stabbed at the waters of the Ganga. Ganga guided the hands of the soldiers, who were horrified by the sight and sound of the trumpeting, bleeding giants. The cries of those gentle hearts swept across the full range of the world's music. When they ceased beating and the river was red, bursting with the creative spirit lodged in their memory, the elephants sank beneath the waves.

Ganga had kept her word. Chuharmal was avenged.

▼

Their lamentations went around the planet, shrouding the Mountain. The deodars lowered their branches to receive them. Catkins and cones persuaded thousands of mammals to mourn the slaughtered giants beloved of Ganesha's father, Shiva. Informed by Dauna, Kushuma and Reshma, the Malins of Mithila joined their magical powers to cover the slopes of the Himalayas in hibiscus blossoms. The Mountain sparkled like a ruby, like the burning gem that had jammed into Chuharmal's chest beneath his metal breastplate when he stabbed Bhuranand; nothing would ever extinguish its flames. Divine energy went on animating all cosmic manifestations, endlessly projecting and absorbing them, indifferent to putrefaction and ashes.

▼

"May Chuharmal and his soldiers go on their way," a broken Salhesh murmured. "Each of us goes towards liberation at his or her own pace."

He had seen his companions emerge one by one from the reeds, half-fish, half-reptiles, slimy with pitch-black silt... all but the mahouts, who had drowned with the elephants, hanging on to their ears. The effort of gathering his thoughts used up what was left of his strength. He let himself drop to the riverbank and stretched out full length where he had fallen, like a poor man, muttering vague prayers, wild hands clawing towards the water, snatching at the empty wisps of beings in the bloody sponge of the soil.

Much later, when he summoned his companions and their wives to the tree, he refused to use a rostrum. They approached, crouching around him doubtfully, huddled close, men and women clinging to each other as on wedding carpets of interwoven fibres.

"Let us not lose faith," he said at last. "The divine power is entirely free: it binds and unbinds as it sees fit."

Alas, would he serve up only those tired words? He searched for others, but didn't have time.

"What difference does it make?" a merchant grumbled, adjusting the cloth wrapped around his head, "The bridge would never have borne the weight of all those beasts anyway."

He stood up and, without further ado, turned to his stall. Salhesh knew that others would follow suit. At first it would mean just a few gaps in the tapestry of their alliance of goodness, but eventually it would tear.

A few more were about to follow the merchant's lead, their moustaches raised to the sun that gazed upon the scandal in the river, stabbing its rays into their skulls.

"How do we even know you're a good leader, Salhesh?" an emaciated man wearing a leather belt cried out, waving his arms. "At least we could see what Chuharmal was capable of."

He shook his fist and pushed away his wife, who was clutching at him. "May each of them awaken to their own greatness," Salhesh was thinking, "rather than believing in the greatness of another lame one!" But he didn't respond to the insult, and since no one stood up for him, the man sat down. Silence weighed on the assembly, all staring at their implausibly calm guide. If he said nothing, it was surely because he was conversing with the elephants in his mind. But the people waited, he didn't budge, and the heat was pushing everyone to the point of nausea. The men crowded under the banyan tree to get a bit of shade. Some started to chat, others to chew betel or to yawn. Mothers remembered their homes, their animals, their children. No signs seemed to be falling from the sky, nothing since the nightmare of blood. The man in the leather belt suddenly shoved his way to the front row, his wife clinging to him.

"How do we even know you're a leader?" he challenged Salhesh in a harsh voice.

Taken aback, Salhesh nodded, mindlessly picked a leaf from the tree, and walked towards the man, gesturing to Moti Ram and Budeshwar not to follow. The man expressed his anger by kicking his wife. "You didn't arm us!" he shouted. "Crazy man! Triply crazy!"

He turned towards the others, inveighing against the horrors they had witnessed and punching the air over their heads. But the crowd parted before Salhesh like stalks of wheat in the wind's path, and the curses dried up in the angry man's mouth. The leather thongs that held up his ragged clothes showed that he wasn't a peasant. They labelled him as someone who dismembered dead cows, who was taunted even by those who cut pigs' throats and ate rats. He was less than a peasant. He was the muck stuck to the feet of the dregs of the earth.

When the crowd of companions got a good look at him, one of them, a goldsmith, told Salhesh, "Don't waste your breath on those who stink of putrid meat. That fool should keep his foul mouth shut."

Then the throng brought the king and the impure together, and the king didn't mind. He saw all of the world's filth rising up around them, its sweating, sour matter; grumbling intestines; hundreds of fiercely open mouths; and once again he withdrew into himself. This time, he could perceive crushing fear all around him, at the base of all existence. Even the best among them allowed their inner coward to step on their neighbours at the first chance, for nothing but the illusory impression of hoisting themselves above their own indigence. Any moment now, these people who had once believed it advantageous to follow him would be hungry. They might cross the bridge with him, but the men would still disdain their wives and yearn to thrash them, to beat others, feed this appetite for cruelty. So he let his hand float over the crowd from one side to the other, drawing them all in. Noticing the amulet the ostracized man wore around his neck, he spoke to him warmly as to a close relative.

"Like you," he said thoughtfully, "I place my trust in Durga."

"The goddess protects me from snakes," the man growled, disconcerted.

"Does Durga protect your wife, too?" Salhesh asked.

"Maybe," the man replied, sounding uneasy.

Sniggering broke out around them, and Salhesh shuddered. The oafishness was going to swell and swell until it burst in his face. Then the sky would regurgitate its hail and storms over this humanity that smelled like rotted meat. "Lord," he prayed silently, "You see that we are powerless to stick to our noblest intentions. Please help me! It's urgent, if I may say so."

He began to breathe deeply, and his heart expanded. Amid this he could see the dreamer he was, still wallowing in his ideals. The others could hear him moaning. Believing him unwell, three women rushed up. Was the problem from above or below? Squeezing past the crowd, the three peasant women reached him and placed a garland of flowers around his neck. He raised his head, standing straight in the midst of his companions, their souls pillaged. His gaze spread over them all, limpid, almost terrifying, and came to rest on the unloved man with the leather thongs.

"Here, take this," he said, as he handed one woman

the leaf of the banyan still clasped in his hand.

"As the heavens and the earth are my witness," he declared in a powerful voice, "know that you are blessed."

Trembling, she obeyed. Then he added softly, so that only she could hear, "Go to the riverbank, lean down and gather a drop of water from the Ganga in this leaf."

He let her go, his gaze travelling first to her husband, then to the crowd, to get them to follow her to the banks of the river that was flowing, curdled with sorrow, to the sea. A silence filled with hateful incomprehension fell over his companions. They huddled instinctively around the distrustful goldsmith who had no desire for their approach or their ill-tamed presence. What honour fell to the male and female Untouchables? The squalid and the foul! Till it stirred the imagination, the mark of respect seemed misplaced and horrifying.

Yet the emaciated man was walking a few paces behind his spouse, and the crowd followed them, their rancour sharpening with each step.

At that moment, Salhesh was free of both thought and desire. The scribe who was observing him noted that he didn't know what he was doing.

Instead of the gathered companions, he soon saw, as though from above, the body of a great serpent gleaming in the sunshine, and he recognized himself in the agile silhouette that slithered alongside the reviled couple. His soul hovered on the cusp of day and night. Beneath him, scales were falling off, some sparkling, others dull, and the men and women reappeared with their angry faces.

They crouched along the riverbank, still hoping for a revelation that was taking its sweet time, suspecting that Salhesh had ridiculed and hoodwinked them, humiliated them further by having these dog-eaters, whose very shadow should never touch their own, pass before them. They stayed, clinging to their need to see the vile ones dispatched to oblivion, and the cow-skinner charred to death. When everyone had taken their place, the king ordered the Chandala's wife, "Use this banyan leaf as a cup, and scoop up some water for us!"

Then Salhesh floated back down into his body, and addressed the crowd, "Open your eyes to the sacred river Ganga!"

The instant the leaf grazed the water's surface, the river turned green from source to sea.

"Water lentils!" the man with the cow-skin belt shouted, as an immense clamour spread through the crowd, infecting both the Brahmin and the young.

"What are you waiting for, young woman" Salhesh asked with shining eyes. "Can't you catch even a single lentil in your leaf?

She plunged it in the water, but the tiny speck she brought out swelled so quickly that the leaf bent under its weight. Up and down the river, seven hundred lentils imitated the first one, turning into huge grey pearls.

"The elephants!" the stunned crowd began to shout. "And here come the mahouts, too!"

"Praise be to you, Lord," Salhesh murmured in boundless gratitude. Bhuranand was waving his trunk and flapping his ears amongst flocks of birds, thousands of passerines and skimmers that had suddenly appeared out of nowhere to salute the miracle.

When three ghostly silhouettes emerged from the grey froth to bow before him, he recognized the peasant women who had brought him the garland of flowers, and scrutinized their faces. Dauna, Kushuma and Reshma, the kind-hearted sisters, appeared in their essence, and he finally understood the importance of feminine energy, because their magic stemmed naturally from their intimacy, and was the fruit of their faith in infinite cosmic generosity.

Filled with wonder, Salhesh was thinking, "May it please the heavens that distress transports me to attain this intense freedom in my heart! May my self dissolve so that I regain this fusion with eternal felicity!"

Still, sensing that he risked losing his companions, he thanked the Malins warmly, and focused his mind on the journey to the Mountain.

"Do you think we'll really reach Mount Meru, Karikant?" Anil whispered, observing Salhesh as he joined Heeraman and his brothers under the banyan tree. "Will we really found a society of freedom, justice, and brotherhood?"

Karikant tipped his head to one side and bit his lip. "Heeraman thinks Salhesh will reach the Mountaintop," he said. "He says that he has never found him lacking in goodness. But he also thinks that his experience as a guide is insufficient. For instance, the fact that Salhesh refuses to allow the sexes or castes to be separate in his model society... Heeraman says it's rash."

"What about you, Karikant, what do you think?" Anil pressed him, his brow furrowed.

"I agree that it's rash, because not everyone acts in good faith. Not to the extent that he does. Not as constantly. And that makes all the difference."

Pensive, Anil watched Salhesh stop in the huge shadow of the banyan tree to speak to the scribe, who had his stylus and tablet in hand. The tree was like a sitar, with its melodic strings that could vibrate to the finest solicitations of his voice.

"But Salhesh has a magic weapon," Karikant added. "People don't know this."

Anil closed his eyes to concentrate.

"Pashupata, Shiva's weapon, the weapon of the mind and the word. Aligning thought, word, and action," Karikant curbed his enthusiasm as he went on. "Salhesh's power comes from what the vulgar scorn about him: his innocence. He maintains himself in the original divine energy, refuses to let himself be perverted or distracted, not even by his own sorrows. There is no other secret."

"Even when Chuharmal slaughtered the elephants?" Anil asked, his brow troubled by the flocking images.

"Well, there are circumstances..." Karikant admitted, embarrassed.

The red vision broke his stride. But he kept trying. "Listen, I'm telling you what I understood, and you'll have to settle for this for now. What matters is to reside in truth, that's the primordial power. There's nothing else. In the beginning, there's life: that is to say, the intention. Light is shed on it. Then each of us, at our own level, we shine our little light on the intention, and do our best to stay aligned."

In response to Anil's look of doubt, Karikant concluded in a rush, "It's a freedom there for the taking. He took it. Breaking with all of our preconceived notions and prejudices, our conditions of existence, the categories imposed by external causes—it's a choice, though it may seem to be killing him. I can't add to this, Anil. Salhesh is a genius, I'm telling you."

5

Anil didn't always understand Karikant, but he hesitated to strike up a conversation with boys his own age. He was jealous of their sacred threads, even though they had renounced them. Knowing they had repudiated their entitlements after meeting Salhesh, he could sense that there was something admirable about them; something that at the same time he didn't feel like admiring. The absent thread cast a sanctifying glow over them, like a halo. It took its place among desirable objects in Anil's mind—and came to define his horizons as much as the possibility of reaching the Mountain. What if the Mountain should evaporate in the same way as these spoilt boys' access to an elevated caste. What if the Mountain turned out to be one more mirage.

The thrumming of doubt had a different effect on those young men. They were disinclined to acknowledge qualities in Anil whose basis they couldn't yet fathom. Salhesh had rejected the traditional social order, but in favour of a lucidity that had hardly been established. Granted, the Brahmins weren't really born from the head of Brahma, the god of creation; the boys had let go of that flattering legend. But that a callow little linnet-head like Anil could converse with the divine spirit as easily as they, as though it were perfectly natural—this was carrying the principle too far.

The Revolution of Love was going to take a while.

With Salhesh, all that was strange floated lightly upon his convictions and didn't seem to pose a problem. Everyone else found it troubling, and for the same reason, fascinating.

▼

"What does the Journey mean, Salhesh?" Anil asked later, when he brought him his spiced milk.

"It means transformation," Salhesh replied. "Seven hundred men have heard my call to form a new society, and seven hundred women have joined them. They have returned to their homes tonight, to hand their responsibilities over to their families, and will be back tomorrow. Then we will cross the bridge that is as flimsy as a wisp of straw—two elephants a day, don't worry, no more than that. Yes, you heard right... It will take a year."

Dumbstruck, Anil dropped the spices and stammered, "Even in the months when Vishnu is sleeping? When he lets the demons run riot over the world? Even during the four months when we're in the hands of the nocturnal powers?"

Salhesh frowned. "You can chant hymns in Vishnu's honour and we can plant basil. You can worship him however you please, my young friend, with rice and vermilion if you like; but we won't fear the nocturnal powers. The rainy season spreads over the Himalayas just as it does where we're from: we'll fast, and by the end, we'll feast on yam roots and peas. But keep our bridge in your mind, Anil."

The boy bowed low. Salhesh traced an arc in the air.

"A bridge... between the old world and the one that we are going to build in the shelter of the white wall of the Mountain. On the other side, we'll build a village, one house at a time, to welcome all comers. We'll build them with elephant dung. We'll all work together, learning from each, regardless of our origins, profession or sex."

Anil bowed still lower.

"And if our community has a king, his role will be to serve everyone," Salhesh concluded.

"Will I be able to worship the moon when it's full," Anil asked, "and offer her a dish of dal at the right time?"

"You'll do as you please, Anil," Salhesh replied. "But think about our bridge."

Wiping his brow, Moti Ram sat down near them. He had just gone around the whole camp with Budeshwar. The mahouts had found neither fresh wounds nor scars on the elephants' bellies. Not the slightest trace of violence on their bodies; their peaceable gaze unchanged.

"Our people won't all follow you, Jaybhardan," he said, mixing spinach and onions in a banana leaf. "Your words moved them, but they didn't really understand."

"Don't forget to point out that the words frightened them," Salhesh said, without reacting to the deliberate use of his former name, the name of his youth.

"Your words frightened them," stated Moti Ram.

"Do go on."

"For many people, their condition isn't even the hardest part..."

Anil was trying to follow this train of thought.

"The hardest part would be changing it... Even if the landowners take advantage of them, and thrash and rape their women," Salhesh concluded for him. "What my brother says is true, Anil."

The boy nodded without understanding very much, his gaze dull and strange, and himself on the verge of falling to pieces, of dissolving. Moti Ram wiped his mouth with the back of his hand.

"Then what? Let's say that our people are too scared to attempt your revolution. Tomorrow morning, they won't be seven-hundred-strong any more..."

"Very well," Salhesh said. "Let's suppose that tomorrow, there will be only seventy, including the women. Or only seven or eight..."

Anil turned anxiously to Karikant, who had remained silent until now.

"Couldn't the women decide to come on their own?" he asked. "You want to restore their dignity. You've tempted them!"

Salhesh nodded in agreement. "The women will decide for themselves."

Moti Ram looked to Heeraman for support, but the scribe was absorbed in the task of capturing their adventure for posterity, under a title chosen by the guide himself: The Journey. Moti Ram leapt up, upset and full of recriminations.

"But you're talking about a reality that doesn't exist! The picture you're painting tempts them as paradise tempts us."

Salhesh brought his hands together and considered what he'd said. Then, turning to the scribe, he asked, "What do you think, Heeraman?"

The latter looked up from his task, embarrassed.

"The Ancients warned us," he replied prudently. "They said, 'Men whose families are not ruled by order have a home guaranteed in hell.'"

"We shall leave them their heaven and hell, my friends," Salhesh spoke quietly, taking up a clay cup filled with warm milk. "Let us be content to practice the modesty and honesty that the Ancients also advised, along with non-violence, which is essential. Non-violence, and the detachment of the self..."

"Pardon me, Salhesh," Moti Ram shot back. "Detachment is all very well and good. But there may be an obstacle. What if the people love you too much?" He put it another way, "How can one abstain from attachment to you?"

"By attending to Consciousness," Salhesh replied, lowering his eyes to spare them both. "It is the condition of our liberation. Consciousness and transformation... That is our journey."

Moti Ram brushed him off impatiently. "Where are you leading us, King Salhesh?" he whispered sorrowfully.

Salhesh raised his eyes, allowing Moti Ram a full view of his face as he queried the bewildered ones of his closest companions, one after the other.

"I am talking about an inner journey, from the self to the Lord," he replied without raising his voice. "All the way to an absolute bond: identification with all things."

Moti Ram exploded again, nostrils flaring and eyebrows arching up to his temples. "A journey to nowhere!" he exclaimed. "Do you mock us? If you invoked Pundra and Shambhala, the fabulous regions of the old legends, we might at least be heartened! After all, isn't that where you're leading us, near Mount Meru, in the Himalayas?"

Salhesh put his cup down to take his brother's hands in his, but Moti Ram hardened himself to Salhesh's touch, a block of stone. He went on vehemently, "You're trying to be a saint! Do you want them to idolize you? Veneration or hatred: the people know nothing between the two. It seems like you're polishing your statue the better for them to break it later."

The others were aghast. Anil expected demons to assault them at any moment.

"The fabulous regions designate the Mountain, the axis of the world and the source of all happiness," Salhesh went on as though he hadn't noticed anything amiss. "For now, let us work on our own righteousness; let us make it fertile. Therein lie the meaning and purpose of every single day of the journey, and therein lies our paradise, even if the bridge were to collapse tomorrow under the weight of the first of our elephants. And if, one day, my person were to become an obstacle..." At that, he stopped and stared at his brother with impressive clarity before bowing before him—"...it will disappear. I solemnly swear it before you, Moti Ram."

Baffled, Heeraman nearly dropped his stylus.

"For our society... What should I note down, Salhesh? It has to be summed up."

"You're right, Heeraman, let's sum things up: we will all be peasants. We will till the land together."

He spread his hands wide, paused, and drew an imaginary vertical line.

"And each of us in their own place will be responsible for their own acts, here and now."

"You were talking about an axis," Heeraman objected, looking down, "but now you're drawing a cross..."

"Of course," Salhesh replied. "Just imagine the concentration of energy at the critical point, my friends: Consciousness. The simplest and most efficient plan is there. For our community."

▼

Bhuranand was running his trunk over his fellow elephants to make sure they were unharmed while he waited for Salhesh near the bridge. The women were chatting in one group, and the men in another. Salhesh sighed quietly, and Anil yearned for the childhood he had left behind.

Later, Salhesh had a conversation with the boy, to further his education.

"You have to know how to take risks, Anil," he said gently. "When you believe in the invisible, you try many different things."

Anil nodded.

"Has anyone ever called you a wimp or an idiot? Don't believe a word of it. Test yourself. But you have to know how to resist others. Take us, for instance. We are close to each other, and perhaps you hold me in a certain esteem. But you still don't have to follow me. You can resist my influence."

Anil didn't know how to interpret that, so Salhesh went on, "You could go back to Mahisautha. Not only are you free to do that, but in a way... how can I put this? ... It doesn't make any difference to me."

Seeing how dismayed the boy looked, Salhesh corrected himself, adding in a neutral voice, "I mean that it's none of my business. Do I hold any authority over your conscience? For your part, I wish only for whatever your conscience—after having carefully weighed the pros and cons—believes is most beneficial to you."

The next day, seventy companions showed up. Sixty women and ten men were ready to embrace the unknown, or offer themselves a chance to experience reality directly and without artifice.

6

They crossed the bridge in due course. The whole operation was spread over three months since the number of companions was smaller than expected. Moti Ram and Budeshwar brought up the rear on their horses, having entrusted the extra elephants to the care of those householders who had decided to stay behind. They met their peers in the shelter of a nearby forest so as not to attract Chuharmal's attention.

Vishnu was starting to let the demons run wild over the world, but on the other side of the river, the companions were discovering more and more advantages to industrious cooperation every day.

Under the banyan tree, Anil dithered endlessly, unable to decide whether to follow them or not. He prayed, cried, and fasted, grappling with his doubts about humanity's mettle in tests of fortitude—irresolute as people were, and unsatisfied, neglecting to cultivate endurance in adversity, and encumbered with minds that wallowed in childishness. Trapped in the web of memories, he watched men and women borne up by enthusiasm cross over to the other side. Nothing frightened them: not Chuharmal's acolytes who infested the area, not Chinese invaders, or tigers, or the future. When Salhesh's brothers left, Anil finally understood that by caressing bits of dead time, he was losing out on life itself. He raised his eyes to the treetop, glimpsed the sky beyond the branches, and dashed across the bridge as speedily as a well-nocked arrow. He was the last one across.

Salhesh welcomed Anil on the other side, sitting in a circle of women, cradling a baby. Chuharmal's son.

7

Clouds slowly coiled and released themselves from around the Mountain, barely grazing the cedar sentinels that guarded the ice diamond. Krishna spoke.

"They're taking the leap, Shiva. Are you proud of your champion? He's destroying the old world without seeming to touch it."

"He does fight. He resists the weight of external pressure and brings human questioning inwards. After all, in essence, true consciousness is action."

"A king without a kingdom or an army," Krishna added. "His government isn't going to look like much."

"That's exactly what I'm hoping for: that it will look like nothing anyone has seen before. Let him try. He's encouraging women and men to explore their inner resources and, at the same time, universal sharing. The King of the Mountain is shaking things up. Reviving them. Powers are unfolding."

"You'll never change, Shiva!" Krishna joked. "You love chaos."

"Yes to astonishment," Shiva shot back. "Yes to wonderment."

"What will become of our cults?"

"You can't complain! Salhesh doesn't stop anyone from honouring Vishnu, whom you represent. Vishnu the Preserver."

"And you, the Destroyer."

"I sow revolution. I regenerate," Shiva retorted. "Salhesh is clairvoyant. He modifies and balances in complete awareness of *the nature of both man and the world."*

"*It's true that consciousness is the creative force of the universe,*" *Krishna replied, playing with the wind.*

"Chuharmal's son," Salhesh repeated. "We don't know who his mother is, and his father abandoned him for an alliance with the sovereign of China. He rode away with his horsemen, the baby's wet nurse told me. 'We're headed for Lalitpur, the city of beauty,' I replied. 'Come with us. We'll take good care of you and the baby.'"

Anil stared at the women sitting around him. In the centre of their circle, Salhesh was rocking the child as though it were the most natural thing to do. Why didn't the wet nurse sitting by him move somewhere out of sight?

Salhesh sensed his discomfort.

"In your opinion, my dear Anil, does it make sense to humiliate those who give life?"

"It's done, I believe," the boy answered, "because they are said to be impure."

"What's done is to subject them to ritual precautions, as though they must make up for some imaginary stain through blind devotion to their husbands, and that doesn't bother you?"

"I don't think so," Anil said hesitantly.

"What if you took a better look at those who are called impure? Women, Dusadh, Chamars, Doms, Musahars and so many others... Where do you think they should be cast out? We must be wary of ideas, Anil. Look at faces instead. We are all one family. Let's leave ideas to others, and let's go towards life, which doesn't categorize, but tends to allow everything to blossom."

Seeing how confused Anil looked, Salhesh handed the infant back to the wet nurse and reached his hand out to the boy.

"Come sit under our tree with us, my son," he said.

They walked over to the pipal tree Salhesh had selected for speaking to the companions. Salhesh was thinking about his mother, Madoderi, who was no longer alive; and about the other woman who had welcomed him into her womb, who was now under Somdev's protection; about the midwife chased away by his counsellors: rumour had it that she had been kidnapped by bandits.

His discourse followed the same slope that his thoughts were already rolling down.

"Submission to the husband—be it genuine or feigned—withers women," he expounded to the crowd which contained women emancipating themselves and men allowing it. "But that's not all. It deprives the universe of their generous sensuality, and, I might add, of their spontaneity."

Not all of the companions knew what that meant. With his writing table set on his crossed legs, Heeraman took note of this detail.

Salhesh went on, "In addition to desirable austerities, speculative wisdom, and sacrificial intentions, it is a must that the little spark in the heart... should gleam! And flash! We're going to see great wreaths of lightning, my children."

The King of the Mountain sometimes got so carried away that he wasn't easy to follow. But a general sense of what he was getting at came through, and his audience was rewarded for its patience.

"Women's spontaneity tastes like unblemished fruit when it connects with the breath of cosmic life, my friends," Salhesh went on. "Without it, the world grows tough, and is considerably impoverished."

He let his companions dwell on those last words before going on, "Just as the sun doesn't distinguish between those who are good and those who are evil, between Brahmins, dogs and stones; couldn't we air our minds out from time to time and bathe them in freedom? Let unity inspire us!"

Ponderous silence was the only response.

"We're going to blow everything up," he added, thrilled. "Non-violently, of course: our revolution doesn't kill, it embraces. I meant that we would blow up grammar and definitions."

The Invisible Ones flocked under the branches, followed by miniature monkeys clinging to each other's tails. Hanuman was the god of grammar, yes or no? The scribe focused on his tablet.

Salhesh was going too far. The people weren't following him, their attention was wandering.

"Nonetheless, we must attend carefully to our integrity," Salhesh added swiftly. "We must not cut ourselves off from anything, not exclude anything or anyone, not dismember ourselves. We will touch what is perishable and liable to rot, low things, and we shall meet the stars. Let's try to live in a fundamental cosmic brotherhood."

Had he hammered it in sufficiently? "None is impure, all are divine." He caught his breath and dove back in, "Integrity will offer us the world as a whole, instead of an annoying mash. Let us be honest and acknowledge this truth: impurity doesn't exist."

He wiped his brow with a corner of his tunic. Even through the leafy canopy, the sun pounded on their heads. He knew perfectly well that his teaching exhausted them, but he remained convinced it was his duty to massage their intelligence as a wet nurse massages a newborn's muscles. The words had to be repeated, over and over, so they would penetrate the scalp like oil, easing in here, caressing there, wrapped in a song that carried the message to the universe. Even if they didn't assimilate every single detail, it would do. What he had drummed into their heads would sprout and bloom.

By the time he had finished, most of the women, and the men, had dozed off. Anil too, but this time he was dreaming of a day when his mother and father would no longer be insulted and spat on.

They journeyed on through storms and upheaval. The god of wind drew up a huge mass of air, born of the sea's long patience and heavy undulation, now rolling overhead in blasts of wind and rain, nature's compelling force. North of the plains of Ganga, the companions wordlessly yearned for monsoon. While relatives back home were overwhelmed with the work of harvest, the journeyers realized that they missed the rice-growing season keenly. They craved the touch of seedlings, yearned for greenery and the sensation of standing barefoot in rice paddies. They had dreamt of creating new seed cultures in the Himalayas, but the wind here abated only to return and batter anew the flank of the mountain, riffling its soil and probing between rocks, raking the water held in its folds, leaving the new inhabitants grieving for their missed rice harvest.

"You will see what no one has ever seen," murmured Salhesh, who guessed their thoughts. "You will experience what no one before you has known: a society free from the scales and partitions that have befallen us without justice or respect. The world needs you to bear witness."

As they marched onwards, his words became rarer and gained in weightiness. He remained confident, and never neglected to converse with them. He also took time to listen to the inhabitants of the places they travelled through, inquiring after the threats the monsoon posed each year. They described how the ground slid from beneath their homes, carrying away people and animals alike; the curse of flooding that destroyed crops; as well as the beautiful white rice, that marvel beloved of the Lord. Salhesh's courtesy ripened into compassion. They would pray together, each in their own way. When the suffering populace needed to be saved from mudslides, Bhuranand and his other elephants would carry them to shelter in the high rocks. Salhesh's face glowed, and everyone was surprised by his gentle firmness. There was something extravagant about his words, but his confidence made them irresistible.

The flow of his discourse also smoothed over not a few gaps in his plan. Salhesh didn't let on even to those closest to him that he didn't actually know where he was leading them, and he started by avoiding thinking about it. The revelation would take place in the fullness of time. They had left behind the men and women they had been, left the old burdens with them. They were revealing themselves, unfurling as they journeyed. This was wonderful in and of itself. He invited them to yield, as he had, to an indeterminateness that could not last. His mind happily emptied itself of all hypotheses or projections, to such an extent that the emptiness itself tempted him more than the noblest of goals would have. He had had the feeling before, but never as frequently as under the clouds crowning the Mountain.

Most of the people they came across assumed they

were pilgrims, heading to the banks of the river Bagmati to honour Shiva Pashupati, lord of the animals. Salhesh neither confirmed nor denied anything. He would explain their project: brotherly love extended to all beings, and in fact to the Earth itself. He would explain that, although he was a king, he hardly ruled. A natural balance of strengths and attributes would be the true master. Each would be responsible for their share. To those who bemoaned his unmarried state he would reply, "Harmony will be our queen," with a smile so wide and empty that it erased the edges of his own being. The people he spoke to looked at each other, many hesitated, and some abandoned everything to follow him.

▼

By the time they arrived at Janakpurdham, the companions numbered seven hundred once more, or perhaps even seven thousand. Monsoon was unleashing itself over the region that had experienced the happy glory of Janaka, the king who had renounced worldly illusions. Janaka was the father of Sita, wife of the great Rama. Salhesh discussed the power of the law with him. Sheets of water crashed all around them, ripping up trees and covering villagers in mud, sweeping away houses and livestock. While the water washed over them, he named Janaka as his model because he had renounced illusions about worldly possessions and preferred to instil goodness in the hearts of others. Janaka had been close to the sage

Ashtavakra, whose name meant 'the Man of Eight Bends' because his body was afflicted with eight disabilities. Ashtavakra was a descendant of the philosopher Aruni, who had studied the nature of reality by observing the world's incessant change.

The people listened as Salhesh related the tribulations of the inhabitants of the marshy terai who, despite everything, continued to raise their eyes to the crystal of the Mountain. Frightened by the violence of the water as the elements raged around them, some of the companions felt incapable of continuing the journey and wanted to go home.

"Chuharmal is waging war against the local kings, hoping for China's support," Salhesh replied. "He now sees us as insignificant and inoffensive. What do you fear from the elements when the people here defy them?"

"You try our patience by having us live without weapons," they snapped back. "But even if we don't perish at the hands of Chuharmal and his band, discipline of the mind alone won't save us from other ills. The gods you seem to ignore will want revenge. We shall perish from the cold of night, and by day, serpents will coil in the wounds of our broken bodies."

"Return to your homes in peace, my friends," was all Salhesh replied. "We love you, and we understand you."

He turned towards his brothers, querying them with his gaze. Moti Ram and Budeshwar understood those who went back, that was certain. Perhaps they were even tempted to follow them, but Salhesh had an intuition that the further they progressed towards the Mountain, the more the effort towards liberation meant to them. "The time will come when even attachment to the effort will no longer exist," he promised.

▼

Moti Ram and Budeshwar had to admit, however grudgingly, that having seen Salhesh repair souls in tatters, and those souls repair others, had changed them. They had grown accustomed to seeing him speak to women, and knew that several men of good character who had joined their ragtag group held him in higher esteem than if he had led an army. However unlikely and unexpected it seemed, dialogue—awkward but worthwhile—had sprung up between those who had been incompatible not long before. It emerged from inconceivable moments of sharing, in a bittersweet evolution that depended on a revealed conception of the world: the two brothers were unaware of any precedent to this miracle. They had come, however timidly, to believe in the life they were gradually inventing in this new community, a better life for the children born in it.

At first, everything went pretty well amongst the companions who had heard Salhesh's call in their own conscience. Each man, each woman, was nurtured, in a sense, by their own inner light. But things took a turn for the worse when they began to introduce comparisons among themselves, supposedly to enact the principle of equality that the community was meant to apply. Salhesh had knocked down the walls that divided humanity into higher and lower classes. And now, those who had been ignored for so long were demanding equal regard, and they were doing so with fierce pain in their hearts, because a dormant desire within them had been stirred up. Salhesh had to deal with the inevitable vexations, many of which were instances of wounded pride that required sorting out under the council tree. A few shrewd people whispered that there was nothing surprising here: a society in mutation was bound to be at greater risk while Vishnu slept.

When the third month had passed, the companions' thoughts turned to preparing the waking-up rituals for the gods. Anil was musing about the dal he wanted to offer the moon, while the women were figuring out where to place their lamps along the river. If the demons had caused little harm to Salhesh's flock, it might be because no one had eaten any meat during that perilous period.

Salhesh never ate any, and he fasted often—but without entirely neglecting the feast days and rituals that encouraged the divine powers to protect the community. When it came to relating to the divine, he leaned towards a nebulous sort of responsibility that was both intimate and communitarian, something he advocated passionately.

He had a knack for jabbing the needle of honour right at the spot people didn't want plumbed. For the most part they would have preferred to uphold the old, well-defined distinctions and separations: between castes, between men and women, and between the sacred and the everyday. All the time. Those closest to him had to remind him repeatedly that it was far easier for people to become absorbed in concerns about the purity of their utensils than to leap into the liberating bath he was offering.

"An acid bath," Karikant commented one day. "Aside from you, Salhesh, who could withstand the test of truth?"

"Is this really the right time to tell our companions about conquering their freedom," Moti Ram added, "when they're still clinging to their folk tales? At the foot of the Mountain, they're still frightening each other with stories about cross-eyed demons and goddesses who can never sate their hunger for human skulls. The companions aren't like you, they don't spend all their time exploring their innermost selves. They want you to tell them what to do. You're going too fast for them."

"I would like our words and actions to spring from mature minds..." Salhesh murmured. "We are learning together... We are changing together."

"You're going too fast," Moti Ram insisted, his tears welling. "I know men who still fantasize about butchering their neighbours—and about filling their wives' vases the moment the neighbours' backs are turned."

Salhesh went stock-still in shock. Budeshwar tried to smooth things over, "You are great, my brother, and you sparkle like crystal," he added gently. "But we are stuck in a rut, ripped at by thorns and threatened by wild beasts."

"Rape... murder..." Salhesh stammered with horror, lips pale and hands joined in prayer.

"Well, I may have exaggerated a little," Moti Ram allowed, "but..."

"There are no 'buts', Moti Ram. Go on," Salhesh said curtly.

Budeshwar was pacing back and forth, stroking his moustache. Moti Ram dove in, "A man from Janakpur was complaining about you today, that's what is the matter. Someone was hoeing with a sharp implement, he said, and that was sure to arouse the anger of Maldrozichen, the leader of the Nagas. We shall be surrounded by six-foot-long cobras. They will spread their hoods and bare their fangs..."

"And when Maldrozichen whistles, they will all attack at once," Budeshwar concluded bitterly. "An hour later, we'll all be dead. Farewell, companions!"

"I see," Salhesh replied coolly. "And would you say that the man was actually complaining because I had them start building new homes for poor people who can barely speak, so backward are they?"

"All I'm saying is, according to him, Maldrozichen is going to lash out against us," Moti Ram replied uneasily. "Open your eyes to what we're dealing with every day, Salhesh."

"I see," Salhesh repeated, his face shuttered.

Horrifically unhappy, he withdrew to fast, and night crept over them with chilling slowness.

▼

Just once, he sought comfort from Bhuranand and wondered about the meaning of his royal lineage. Brahmins had consecrated his father's coronation. They had performed rituals that would favour the descent of divine energy upon him, because it was in the very nature of divinity to spread its grace over the world. "Your guru will teach all of you the paths of liberation," Somdev had told his sons later, but one of you will be the receptacle of the most intense grace. He will spontaneously achieve divine plenitude in all of its expressions and will be tasked with leading the others towards practices that will inspire the gradual awakening of consciousness."

The elephant soon leaned over its meditating master. It turned into a vibrating cedar tree, and the wind's song whistled in its branches to remind Salhesh of the perpetual succession of cycles in the visible and invisible worlds. Plunged into that continuity of sound, he could feel the marvellous tree rocking while he floated back to memories of childhood. The teacher in charge of transmitting the sacred hymns to them was scolding his brothers, while he, Jaybhardan, trembled at the thought of making an intonation mistake that might set off a cataclysm. Salhesh smiled at the child's notions, and the tree's branches burst into bloom. Then the Malins appeared before him as young women, and began to unroll their hair in front of him.

"The buns in our hair are nests for thousands of mantras, King of the Mountain," they said. "The wind has buried sacred sounds within them."

Beauty opened to the beyond and invited him to penetrate divine reality. He would perceive for himself the handle of Shiva's trident soaring over his head, with the three goddesses perched on the three prongs—peaceful and white in the centre, hectic and red on the right, furious and black on the left. Yet the Supreme Goddess, whose emanations they were, never revealed herself to novices...

Just as he was feeling ready, the flute-like laughter of the Malins drew him out of his dream. He emerged from it too quickly, half inside it still, half out, confused and embarrassed. They withdrew, giving him time to compose himself; then he joined them by the water's edge.

"Your initiation is not yet complete, Salhesh," they told him. "You are close to identifying with the animating power of the universe, but you refuse one part of its expression: the reception and manipulation of that power through certain rites. Follow us, and you will learn more."

He was instantly wary, and tightened the knot on top of his head; they were joking in a language he didn't speak. Dauna went on, "You reprove the toughest practices, in which sex exerts itself in death, Salhesh. Everything is indeed possible, and not all things are advantageous. But do not fear magic, when all nature is a manifestation of divine energy."

"Will you come with us?" Kushuma asked, strewing sweet-scented petals around her. "Know that we approve of your rule: that none shall treat another person as their tool."

They huddled together, consulting each other in grateful whispers, then bowed before him.

"Will you come with us?" Dauna and Reshma repeated charmingly.

"It would be vain to try demarcating Salhesh's period in the history of mankind," Shiva commented in a faraway voice.

"Weeks, months, and years may well have passed," Krishna replied, "since justice spread in his reign across the valleys of the Ganga and Lalitpur, and even to neighbouring regions."

Shiva agreed.

"For his part, Chuharmal has brought appreciable order to Mokama," Krishna noted.

"Salhesh's elevated mind has done more than just reign over the society of men: it has penetrated it, from Brahmin to outcaste. He has taught men to hold daughters and mothers in esteem, taught them to respect animals and trees. The craving for ownership has receded and brutality along with it. Attentive love is powerful.... It repairs, it edifies. Salhesh was right to try it as a method of government."

"The journey is carried out through bravery and sharing," Krishna intoned. "Travellers exercise their bodies and souls without expectation or appetites."

"Consciousness is radiating," whispered Shiva. "A crystalline light shines through. Salhesh has spread a new awareness of the world across this region. May all beings shine, and each be its own jewel of life!"

"Heeraman's account has been lost," Krishna added, "but does it matter to track relative existences in precise detail? The life-affirming story is true."

"Salhesh's story is true," they breathed together before

vanishing into the air. "It is written in the furrows of Janakpur and in the serpents' nest, in the waters and under the wings of eagles circling the Mountain. May the women of Mithila continue to paint Salhesh's acts and so transmit his wisdom to the world!"

11

They lured him into the den of a priest called Chakranath. In its darkness, he learned that he was neither purity, nor good behaviour, nor veracity.

"You know the spotless fruit of a job well done, Salhesh," they told him, "but you must also cross that circle wherein others feed on ignorance and pain."

He recognized the words of Lord Krishna on their charmed lips, and his memory returned. "And so," he went on, "with the power of free-standing thought, liberated from pride and illusion, victorious over vice and attachment, disencumbered from desire and delivered from pairs of opposites..."

"Delivered from pairs of opposites," Kushuma took over in a hushed tone, "you will achieve the immutable."

"Not sun, moon or fire will ever again illume the place from which you will not return, having once reached it, for released from transmigrations and death..." Dauna added with a sigh.

"It will be your supreme repose" Reshma finished, weakly.

Her voice died out.

Troubled, Salhesh remembered that the great Arjuna had withdrawn from the world to die in the Himalayas, leaving his grandson Parikshit to continue their lunar lineage. Where did he stand in relation to the earth, the sun, and the moon, he who had hoped to dissolve his lineage with the intention of teaching men to disestablish borders within themselves as between one another?

"May the trust that has guided me thus far remain with me," he murmured, as his soul was spattered with a vague, uncertain light.

▼

Crouched between the damp, dripping rocks, they groped their way ahead for some fifty feet, making halting progress. Reshma led, with a candle in her hand. She pointed out holes that looked like entrances to minuscule cells.

"Remember, Arjuna used magical weapons," Dauna whispered to Salhesh.

The passage finally broadened. They came upon a clearing filled with pale smoke. Reshma immediately blew her candle out.

"Conceal yourself in this mist with us," Dauna ordered him in a low voice.

An image crossed Salhesh's mind: the master of the gods filling the sky with clouds to drown the forest in rain. "His" own battle was to commence here and now. He would be strong, liberated, and victorious. He would be detached; he would be delivered. He would rip open seams and overcome obstacles. For the moment, he felt like he was flaking apart... Was his body dissolving into mist, into thousands of drifts? Were his eyeballs multiplying? Was he becoming ether or sand?

In droplets of vision he took the measure of this space.

"We need to focus," Kushuma insisted. "Demons hide in the mist with the gods."

Faint glimmers lit up the rear of the cave where Chakranath was officiating at a ceremony. Salhesh was gradually able to distinguish the fuzzy silhouette of the scrawny, hirsute priest draped in red cloth. His shadow played on the oily slick of the cave walls, bending over rocks, strolling elastically around members of the brotherhood who seemed stuck to the ground, their legs crossed, hands in their laps. Salhesh pictured the brothers focused on compressing the muscles in their buttocks, their senses turned inwards to sublimate their energy and direct it towards the Divine Source. If they weren't careful, they might risk the awakening of desire. A single plume of sperm would spoil everything.

The whole group seemed terrified of the priest. Salhesh opened his eyes wide. One of his old guru's very first lessons came to mind: "Let your breathing infiltrate deep into your body, all the way to the pores on your back!" Holding his breath, he was able to make out small bowls of milk and rice arranged in a ring in the middle of an empty, circular space. At its heart stood a chalice, waiting to receive a precious liquid.

"Offerings for Maldrozichen?" he asked the Malins in a hushed voice.

Their frowns silenced him without a word. The priest vanished, sucked into an invisible chamber. At the back of the cave, blindfolded musicians produced soothing vocal tones. For a brief moment, Salhesh wondered what melodic mode it was, and what its colouration. Perhaps yellow... something close to the shade of egg yolk?

Chakranath appeared suddenly, a few paces away, with a white package in his arms. The music ceased. He laid the package on the ground, by the offerings, and with gleaming eyes launched into a series of mysterious movements that caused his red cloth to flutter like a blaze. The flames caressed his slender shape, hiding, revealing and devouring it in a frenetic cycle that needled the nerves. The gathering of brothers didn't move a muscle. Salhesh felt a trickle of sweat slide between his shoulder blades. Finally, the package unfolded itself, and a terrified, hollow-eyed little girl stood up. The vocalizing started again softly, growing louder. Chakranath ordered the child to dance. Salhesh began to gag.

"Wait and see," Dauna ordered him.

Was it really Dauna speaking in that low voice? Kushuma and Reshma, her delicate sisters? What was their role in this abomination? Why was it the beauty and wonder within them had not recoiled? Was he going mad, accomplice to this foul ritual, this disgraceful sacrifice? His head was spinning from the sight of the haggard child. Mad! Mad! The abominable and the ignominious were humming yellow to distract the scatter-brained fool he was, while pure horror was at work just paces away, which his horrified self did not raise a finger to prevent. Atrocity daubed his soul with red, but the stupefied coward, the defeated one he discovered inside himself was submerged in a diabolical, idiotic sentiment against which his heart struggled valiantly. His body shrieked that he wrest himself away, but the song was howling in his ears, "Veneration!" spinning him around as he offered up gibberish.

At first he didn't see what was slithering across the sandy floor where the little girl was twitching and dancing for all she was worth, jerking like a puppet on a string. The lacquered back of a cobra. His vision blurred with tears, Salhesh barely glimpsed the gleaming chalice in the lap of the priest, who was now sitting among the men nodding their approval of the blood offering to come. Where did the assassin hide his blade? Would he entrust the murder to the venom, and slit the child's throat later, while the brainless herd muttered barely modified sacred spells?

"Clots, stones, and rocks in the flow of the divine word!" he cried out in outrage. "Beauty and awe, what strength is yours in the end?"

Let the others sneer, he screamed in a final outburst of bitterness, "O cave crawling with scrofulous villains! Matrix of death! Must I be swallowed up in the wound where the greatest good and the greatest evil churn together?"

At that, he collapsed into himself, and his soul fled into the night.

The Malins were waiting for him, beyond time and space.

"A smile spreads across his face," Kushuma whispered.

"He has surrendered his attachment to the outside world," Dauna pointed out in a hushed tone.

"He is bathed in tranquillity," Reshma added with relief. "Thinking is no longer an obstacle. He has no more limits. He can penetrate the Supreme Reality."

The three sisters rocked their heads slowly. The supple movement drew the Invisibles along, and a cool breeze ran through the cave.

▼

Having recovered his usual shape and condition, Salhesh didn't have time to ask what pleated fold of reality he had fallen into, or which ingredients of his own nature could have conspired in its emergence. Nor did he have time to consider that it might fuel all sorts of catastrophic demonstrations, whether coherent or unintelligible, and then scatter them in the blink of an eye. When he had recovered the use of his senses, there was no cobra, or Chakranath, nor brotherhood. Just a stream of red hibiscus blossoms at the feet of the little girl, who was playing in the sand while the Malins fussed over her. The empty chalice had fallen amongst the overturned offerings, displaying a golden sun-disk of perfect geometry at its base.

"Has he made it?" Krishna asked.

"Not yet," Shiva replied.

"How long and heavy the time of mankind is," Krishna sighed.

"Salhesh is building a sturdy base for the new society: moral education with a demanding awareness..."

"Appealing to mutual comprehension rather than fear and domination, sharing natural goods..." Krishna went on. "Humanity needs love."

"It needs enthusiasm," emphasized Shiva.

"Educating all these humans will wear Salhesh out."

"Who says he'll be on his own? We are enlisting a woman to achieve his mission."

"In that case," Krishna replied, breaking into a dance. "The neighbouring inhabitants will salute her."

"I am the king of the dance," Shiva retorted. "Salhesh can take his time."

"Then I shall accompany you on my flute," Krishna soothingly responded.

The night was sundered, leaving shreds of dawn in the cedar forest as the clouds thinned out.

"Here he is," whistled the wind.

13

The companions adopted the little girl as readily as they had Chuharmal's son. But when Salhesh announced that they would settle on the plain between two rivers they had never heard of, in the midst of a ring of mountains far inferior in size to Mount Kailash, they protested bitterly. Were the waters of the Bagmati and the Bishnumati really comparable to the Ganga? Why stop mid-route at such an insignificant spot? The companions wanted to climb Shiva's mountain. To seek the axis of the world in its lofty whiteness. They would seek the Meru of their ancestors and settle for nothing less.

They rained scathing criticism down on Salhesh. He replied that the wind swept the flanks of large and small mountains alike. He exhorted them to release their attachment to material things as to their own bodies. But no one had any intention of renouncing their body, and many were the companions who chose to leave at this point. Moti Ram and Budeshwar, however, stuck by him unfailingly.

"Our brother is accustomed to speaking in metaphors," Moti Ram said one day, trying to appease a small group of companions. "When he referred to the axis of the world, for instance..."

"He may actually have been thinking of an inner guideline," Budeshwar hurriedly concluded.

"How so?" they snapped back. "We have been

trudging onwards for months, testing our physical resistance, and just when we are preparing, with bated breath, to climb the Abode of Snow, Salhesh thinks he can eliminate the Mountain with a snap of his fingers? When we've abandoned our old lives for it?"

Several complained bitterly that he had swindled them. They accused him of becoming swollen-headed, of turning into a false prophet. Salhesh didn't close his heart to them. He let them go and embraced the wound they had inflicted. He couldn't reassure or satisfy them. And how could he confess to a world that ran on physical attainments that he himself was made vulnerable by his faith? He would have had to explain that he cherished this opening, of the wound, in the same way as he cherished the openings of his eyes and mouth, or the more intimate one of the Divine Mother.

Nevertheless, inhabitants of the surrounding foothills were drawn to him, spellbound by his edifying words.

"Everything is Consciousness," he would repeat. "Forget the shape of the Mountain. Disregard its appearance, the representations and relations that grip it, and there it is, in the bottom of your heart. It is everywhere. In any place where we become absorbed in the universe we can join the divine energy that is one and free."

When he began to speak of the void as being the same as plenitude, yet more disgruntled companions abandoned him, but again new ones arrived: men and women determined to work alongside him to build a society less in thrall to appearances, less greedy for power and material conquests.

The companions settled more deeply between the two valleys and continued their endeavour for many years, during which they founded families. They were prosperous, and their numbers multiplied.

Salhesh continued to pronounce judgment from under a pipal tree. His brothers, Karikant, Anil and Heeraman seconded him. Visitors from China and Tibet came to consult with him, as well as Brahmin wise men from the Gangetic plains, and women and men from all castes who were curious about his community's social structure. Their children stroked Budeshwar and Moti Ram's horses, and bowed before Bhuranand and the elephants as they would have done to Ganesha and his celestial troop.

Salhesh's reputation reached Mahisautha, enabling Somdev to pass away in peace. His courtiers claimed that the king had never truly recovered from Jaybhardan's defection, that he had lost his mind, but his awestruck subjects also bore witness to the fact that his wrinkled old face became as smooth and brilliant as the pearly petals of a lotus.

After several monsoons, some voyagers appeared on the horizon between two small snowy peaks. The trees in the valley parted to let them pass. Moti Ram and Budeshwar's horses were dead, as were several of the elephants, but Salhesh had just filed Bhuranand's toenails to rounds and placed the sign of Shiva on his forehead.

The travellers were escorting a slightly stooped woman with high cheekbones, whose face was familiar to him. At the sound of her voice, Bhuranand knelt before her. She pointed to the deodars, higher up the Himalayan slopes, and described how, after many tribulations, she had sought shelter with a hermit there, and had served him with great joy. Now that the hermit was no longer of this world, she had come down to the valley to meet Salhesh, whom she had known many years ago in Somdev's court.

Trembling with emotion, Salhesh begged her to go on. She recounted how in the not-so-distant past, Amshuverma, the usurper of King Licchavi Sivadev's power, had reinforced the code that separated groups of human beings from each other, condemning many of them to be scorned by prideful elites. She had heard tell that Salhesh was opposing the caste system, that he intended to restore a code of conduct truer to the original spirit, that he would do so by reintroducing the notion of love into the way of duty. She understood that, thanks to him, there would be no more outcasts or humiliated women. There would be no more Untouchables.

It was Urmila.

Salhesh had a dais of leafy branches built by the riverbank, while he withdrew to meditate alone.

"A sign has been sent to me," he said softly to Anil a moment later. "I will answer it. Please go and fetch my brothers, so they can summon the companions."

When everyone was assembled, he took his place

beneath the pipal tree for the last time, and shared his decision to appoint this wise and warm-hearted woman to his role in the community. The companions were briefly dumbstruck, but he had her brought amongst them and they bowed before her. He then withdrew to the invisible realm, to support from there the former midwife who would henceforth work to bring a healed humanity into the world.

▼

With myriad bewildering events to record in his account of the journey, Heeraman had stopped taking the time to marvel. That day, he took a wide tablet and drew the loving woman: garbed in white, with her braid undone, sitting beneath the Council Tree flanked by Moti Ram and Budeshwar. The dignity of her countenance made her instantly identifiable. Heeraman also managed to sketch Moti Ram and Budeshwar's horses, Bhuranand and the swelling crowd of companions, but he did not portray Salhesh. Salhesh had risen mysteriously into the air. Celestial wonders and a phantasmagoria of colourful birds had preceded his ascension. On the scribe's tablet, in his place, near the woman whom the residents of the Mountain had just accepted, was a space that was empty, or full of light.

AFTERWORD

The Saga of King Salhesh
Martine Le Coz

"A history of Salhesh", painting on paper by Urmila Devi (2019)
Courtesy of Martine Le Coz

I first experienced Dusadh art in 2012 when I visited the village of Jitwarpur, just outside Madhubani town, in the Mithila region of Bihar. The paintings I saw made a tremendous impression on me. I felt a rush of feelings and was left with many questions. The figure of Salhesh was depicted so frequently that I naturally became curious to find out who he was. To my surprise, while many episodes were known, there was no 'complete' written account of his life. Then I met the painter, Urmila Devi, at her home in Jitwarpur. She had such a strong presence. I was moved and enthused by her paintings. This led me to David Szanton, an anthropologist from Berkeley, California, and president of the Ethnic Arts Foundation.

In order to help the Mithila art traditions survive, in 2003, David, along with Parmeshwar Jha with homes in both Madhubani and New Jersey, jointly founded the Mithila Art Institute (MAI) in Madhubani. As president of the MAI, Parmeshwar threw himself into the project body and soul, and later donated half of his own home to the institute. It was there I met Kaushik Kumar Jha, the administrator of the MAI, and Rani Jha (a superb artist and art teacher). In 2014 and 2015, Kaushik Kumar Jha and Rani Jha had shared with me the happy experience of our first collaboration, *Les Filles de Krishna prennent la parole* (Krishna's Daughters Speak), which gathered the testimonies of abased and battered women whom art had enabled to gain a measure of recognition and autonomy. With amazing generosity, both Kaushik and Rani agreed to get involved in this new Salhesh project as well, despite the demands on their time, their professional and personal lives.

Again, in 2017, the three of us teamed up to gather all the existing documents, images, and accounts of Salhesh we could find in order to put his story into writing. We wanted to create both a linear narrative of the saga and to bring this principal and foundational aspect of Dusadh culture to the rest of the world. Despite inevitable gaps and conflicting elements, and no doubt a few errors, the story would be as faithful as possible to the spirit of Salhesh.

For this project, we also engaged Neel Rekha, an art historian in New Delhi with family in Madhubani, who specialized in the evolution of Mithila art. While studying in the Department of Theology and Religious Studies at Leeds University, Neel realized that magic was often a crucial element in Mithila art—as it is in the saga of Salhesh. Later, at Patna University in Bihar, Neel wrote a doctoral dissertation on *Tantrism, Geru, and the Origins of Mithila Painting*. In New Delhi, she in turn invited two scholars from the Bhagalpur Museum, Sunil Kular and O.P. Pandey, to join our research on Salhesh, and they helped to clarify some of the multiple layers of folklore around him.

From the beginning we found that historians did not agree on the dates of Salhesh's reign—sources differ by as much as several centuries—but we settled on the seventh century (Common Era) since Neel had established that it marked the beginning of the Tantric elements in Mithila art, and because its magic played such a large role in the various narratives we collected.

Another key figure in our project was André Padoux, a specialist on Tantrism, who unfortunately passed away in 2017. André opened up this extremely complex domain for me with tremendous goodwill, for which I am infinitely grateful. In his book *Comprendre le tantrisme* (Understanding Tantrism; 2010),[1] he observed that magic has always played a prominent role in Indian culture. With regard to Salhesh, we could add that esotericism, accompanied by magic rites, was firmly established in north-eastern and eastern India at that time with the adoption of Tantric Buddhism or Vajrayana, and Tantric Hinduism. They became particularly powerful forces in the Indo-Nepalese Maithil region of Morang (now a district in the Outer Terai region of Nepal), home of the Malins, magicians who play a key role in the Dusadh saga.

Yet another close associate in the Salhesh project has been Professor Narendra "Nirala" Narain Sinha, Neel Rekha's uncle who lives in Madhubani, who was secretary of the Mithila Art Institute, and in frequent contact with Kaushik Kumar Jha and Rani Jha. As a professor of history at Madhubani's Ram Krishna College and at Mithila University in Darbhanga, he has studied Salhesh's prominence in Mithila art.[2] Based on the presence of the

Vajrayana sect in the region, he confirmed that while there are no "perfect historical proofs", and that although his colleague Rajeshwar Jha, and the eminent Maithili novelist Braj Kishore Verma "Manipadam" had placed Salhesh in the fifth or sixth centuries, it seemed to him that the seventh century was the most likely period of Salhesh's reign given his idealized and magnanimous presence at that time in a wide range of poetic, dramatic, and epic literatures.[3]

Professor Sinha also provided another valuable piece of information: Salhesh's brother, Moti Ram, who became one of the king's commanders, was also a musician, a detail that seemed to confirm Salhesh's role as a divine messenger. In India, it is widely believed and understood that music—as a continuum of sound, words, silence—and gestures, link the creation of the world to Shiva's drumming and dancing.[4] The narratives we know of seldom mention music as one of Moti Ram's attributes, but they all emphasize how powerful Salhesh's words were as he uttered them at the foot of a sacred tree, whether pipal or banyan. The link to Moti Ram's music may help explain their power.

The names of the protagonists in the oral epic often vary from one text to another. We largely relied on George A. Grierson's 1882 partial text in *Maithili Chrestomathy and Vocabulary*.[5] Grierson, for instance, names the King of Pakaria "Bhim Sain", while other authors call him Kuleshar.[6] Grierson's version is not complete, though. He does not, for example, mention

Salhesh's father, while several oral sources identify him as Somdev.

In another version of the epic, Salhesh could turn himself into a parrot named Heeraman, whereas in Grierson, Heeraman is the name of Salhesh's scribe. In a 1978 account provided by Pawan Kumar Jha, then a research assistant at the Master Craftsmen's Association of Mithila, Salhesh turns himself into a parrot, but only to escape the vengeance of Kushuma and her sisters, and avoid succumbing to their charms. In some versions, Somdev's older daughter is granted an important role. Named Bansapti, like the forest divinity, this remarkably intelligent woman is said to have married a prince from Champaran and governed the region for a period in the seventh century.[7]

Although external traces of Salhesh's life are sparse, his internal impulse enabled us to unify his story: he is a guide determined to reform a society plagued by inequality, a man who is both wise and just. Some accounts portray him as a stalwart fighter, with his sword drawn. He is said to have defeated both Chinese and Tibetan armies, with whom his cousin Chuharmal apparently conspired, before returning to Mahisautha and succeeding to his father's throne. As a king, Salhesh is said to have dispensed justice in an exemplary manner: a point on which all the different versions agree.

We preferred an alternative version: that he was a peace-loving and inspiring leader. There is evidence that on several occasions he refused to kill animals, whether during a hunt or for sacrificial reasons. This is a clue: Ashoka had already discouraged hunting in his promotion of dhamma, and had endowed sites of pilgrimage. One of the versions of the story found by Rani Jha shows Salhesh consistently protecting wild animals, with one exception: a jackal that apparently tried to attack a newborn infant. The narrative of his ascension into heaven, or his disappearance into the Invisible Realm, is still passed down by the Dusadh and continues to shed light on Salhesh's extraordinary spiritual dimension.

During our research a "new element" emerged, which confirmed Salhesh's singularity: the Dusadh believe that although he belonged to the social class called Kshatriya, comprising sovereigns and warriors, he chose to withdraw from it to become a poor man. Urmila Devi told this to Rani Jha and me in January 2017 when she welcomed us into her home in Jitwarpur. Her husband Ramvilas Paswan was there in the little courtyard Rani and I knew well by now, along with many family members, including their granddaughter Abhilasha. It was a stunning revelation, incredibly powerful and valuable. Rani had never heard it before, although her enthusiasm for Mithila culture had inspired her to do fieldwork collecting countless songs, chants, poems and narratives. The rebirth of Jaybhardan (Salhesh's birth name), heir to Somdev's throne, as an Untouchable, was a major discovery. Yet we found no trace of it with any of the historians we consulted. This is not too surprising as the Dusadh are Dalits, erstwhile Untouchables, and their culture is essentially little studied by high-caste scholars. Fortunately, Urmila Devi and her husband recounted the episode to us. She also illustrated it with great virtuosity.

▼

Jaybhardan, son of Somdev and Madoderi, king and queen of the kingdom of Mahisautha, went walking in the woods with his younger brothers Budeshwar and Moti Ram. He heard a woman weeping and asked his brothers to help him trace where the sound was coming from. Soon they found a poor pregnant woman and asked her why she was crying.

"I am but a poor, impure woman," she replied. "A worthless person that people insult and spit on. The child I bear will undergo the same humiliations as I, for we are the dregs of mankind."

Jaybhardan, the future Salhesh, looked inquiringly at his brothers. Their mother Madoderi was no longer alive. In an instant, he made up his mind: he would use magic to reduce his body to the size of an embryo and replace the child in the unfortunate woman's womb. In this way, he made himself equal with the humblest of human beings so that the differences between the privileged and the humiliated would vanish.

To tell the entire story, Urmila drew a picture using chiefly green and orange tones. The assembled gods sit in a circle in the centre. All around is a dense forest. Her images don't follow the layout that is customary in

Western art: they must be read from bottom to top and from right to left. On the lower portion of the page we see Jaybhardan astride his elephant, followed by Moti Ram on horseback. Budeshwar is not yet visible; he will appear later. In the bottom right-hand portion, we see the weeping woman with her triangular face, customary in Dusadh art, and a prominent belly. The viewer must accompany the figures along the edge of the sheet, at the bottom, then continue upwards on the left and finish at the upper right. At the lower left; the woman is slimmer now, with three small figures lying near her: Jaybhardan, Moti Ram, and Budeshwar.

On the top left, the young mother expresses her distress to Salhesh when she understands that he is the king's son. "Alas," she says, "I am merely an unworthy creature, a vile Dusadh. What have we done?" She tries to prostrate herself before him, but he holds her up, flinging his bow and arrows (the signs that he belongs to the Kshatriya class of kings and warriors) into a pond. By this gesture, he proclaims that there is no essential difference between human beings, they all form one and the same family. In the centre, the gods witness the entire episode. The last scene shows a single four-headed body comprising the mother and her three sons.

Urmila probably didn't realize how extraordinary her tale was, since it has been circulating amongst the Dusadh since time immemorial.

Another artist from the same community, Shanti Devi, had already illustrated the story of Salhesh in a very vigorous and brilliant sequence of about thirty separate paintings. The Ethnic Arts Foundation has preserved that magnificent work. But Shanti Devi chose to illustrate the episodes in the typical Mithila style marked by 'high' caste aesthetics rather than those of the Dusadh community, which are often considered inferior.

Although the episode of Salhesh's second birth is of crucial importance, it had not been recorded before. It does not appear in Grierson's text, from which we were obliged to diverge, along with the other versions in which his spiritual dimension is expressed only in a magical colouration, the magic being limited to serving ordinary romantic sentiments. Such feelings are incompatible with the Tantric cults that have been practised for centuries in Dusadh lands by means of spiritual possession and extreme transgression. In that tradition, paintings by Dalit women such as Chano Devi and Urmila Devi swarm with dark phantoms. Salhesh would not have been elevated to the rank of a god and would not have become so illustrious were he not charged with potent inspiration.

An already existing motif that finds repetition in Salhesh's story is inter-familial conflict. Towards the end of the narrative Salhesh is forced to confront his cousin Chuharmal, at a time when Salhesh is reaching profound realizations of his own self. In order to achieve the spiritual unity that he had been pursuing throughout the story, he is obliged to recognize what he had overlooked until then: his feminine aspect and the magical forces that are in fact forces of nature. Where Chuharmal believes the Mountain, the physical manifestation of what all characters have been pursuing throughout the story, symbolizes domination of the world of phenomena, Salhesh feels more and more intensely that the Mountain is an invitation to a supreme absorption into the divine. The symmetrical image of their encounter on a bridge—a triangle whose summit points upwards, representing Chuharmal, and a reversed triangle representing Salhesh—illustrates the cosmic field in which creation takes place. The encounter between Salhesh and Chuharmal corresponds to the implicit necessity of a dynamic geometrical order: the triangles intersect each other, symbolizing the transformation of the masculine and feminine principles in the Tantric vision.[8]

The narrative ends on that theme, when Salhesh transmits his governance to a woman. He expresses confidence that she will be able to create enlightened human beings who are attentive to others, and to respect and dialogue with all living creatures in the world. In my retelling of the story, *The King of the Mountain*, I named that woman Urmila, in honour of Urmila Devi of Jitwarpur, who passed the story of her community on to us, in a manner befitting the oral tradition of the Madhubani region.

▼

In order to harmonize the various documents, and to render some of Salhesh's spiritual dimensions, I had to accept that poetical description would make up for certain deficiencies. I also had to accept my own limitations, as well as the sometimes onerous demands of both the research and writing processes. Enthusiasm and emotion needed a large base of confidence to nurture the initial impetus: I was constantly borne up by an unhoped-for and invaluable power: the faith placed in me by Urmila, her husband Ramvilas Paswan and their whole family, as well as by the friends and members of the Mithila Art Institute and of the Ethnic Arts Foundation, most especially David Szanton; Parmeshwar Jha; Neel Rekha and Narendra Narain "Nirala" Sinha; Peter Zirnis and Lina Vincent Sunish; John Bowles, art historian at Radford University, in Virginia; and Hélène Fleury, doctoral candidate at Paris-Saclay University, associate at the Centre for Indian and Asian Studies (EHESS/CNRS) and lecturer in Visual Studies and Preserving Cultural Heritage at Évry-Val-d'Essonne University.

They all warmly welcomed the new friend I soon became, one who had come from France in the footsteps of Yves Véquaud, through whom I learned about Mithila art in the 1970s. I am also grateful to his friend André Édouard, who helped make a connection between Véquaud's work, and David Szanton's and John Bowles's patient ongoing work of collecting and curating works from the Mithila region.

My eternal gratitude towards André Padoux, a demanding and charming guru, can never be adequately expressed. He introduced me to Hélène Fleury, who spontaneously and graciously agreed to read the manuscript of *The King of the Mountain*. I also thank Regan Kramer for her delicate translation of my words into English.

The King of the Mountain is therefore the fruit of a long line of friendship and respect for the ancient traditions of Mithila, in both India and Nepal. I was surrounded by so much goodwill! I want to once again mention the on-site devotion of Rani Jha and Kaushik Kumar Jha, without whom this text would never have come into being, and the warm and friendly help of the family of Mukesh and Sushil Bhati, in both Tours (France) and New Delhi. I thank them all deeply and sincerely.

May the light of the saga of King Salhesh spread over the world.

NOTES

1. André Padoux. 2010. *Comprendre le tantrisme*. Spiritualités vivantes (coll.). Paris: Éditions Albin Michel.
2. *Influence of Folklore of King Salhesh on Harijan Style of Madhubani Paintings, a study in historical perspective – Modern India, Sec.-III.*
3. "Manipadam" authored the historical novel *Raja Salhes* in 1973.
4. François Auboux. 2003. *L'Art du Raga, la musique classique de l'Inde du nord*. Paris: Éditions Minerve.
5. George Abraham Grierson. 2009. *Maithili Chrestomathy and Vocabulary*. Darbhanga: Hetukar Jha and Vedanatha Jha.
6. Rampratap Neeraj and Praful Kumar Maun. 2002. *Raja Salhesh: Sahitya aur Sanskriti*. Muzaffarpur: Namita Prakashan.
7. Ashok Kumar Mehta. 2010. *Lokgathak Nayak Salhesh*. Shambhavi.

8 For more information about the story of Salhesh, see Ajit Mookerjee and Madhu Khanna. 1977. *The Tantric Way: Art, Science, Ritual.* London: Thames & Hudson Ltd.

(Afterword translated from the French by Eleanor Levieux)

OUTRODUCTION

A Triangle Marked by a Dot

This is a story that has been told and retold for centuries, through song and painting, rhyme and colour, rhyming colours and colourful rhymes. Each telling a renewal. This telling, a book, an object of anonymous consumption, in which the story's ancient themes still seem new, its original yearning still unfulfilled—a book about the ideas of a radical personhood, the ideas of a person both legendary and obscure.

This is the book of Salhesh, The King of the Mountain. A triangle marked by a dot.

The story of Salhesh has, for about fifteen centuries, eluded the captivity of the written word. It has not circulated among the powerful, and remains largely outside the circles of power. So when we say he can also be spelt *Salaish, Salahesh, Salhes,* or for those with a yen for diacritics, *Salheś,* it means the written word cannot quite aspire to the subtle equivocations the oral epic has enjoyed. It is a story that has been sung or chanted and performed ceremoniously, in the language Maithili, to the mridang (drum), jhal (cymbals) and harmonium. It is a story that has been painted over and over again. It is a story that resists the idea of an *ur* version, of becoming The Book. Even when it comes bound as a book like the one you now hold, handed to us by Martine Le Coz to whom the master painter Urmila Devi entrusts it, the story remains boundless.

Mysteries must remain mysterious; resolution spells the end of imagination: how and why a writer and artist from Amboise, a small town in central France on the banks of the river Loire that Leonardo da Vinci called home, came to bestow on herself the charge of telling us this semi-historical semi-legendary tale, and how and why did Urmila Devi (and her family of artists), in Jitwarpur village in Madhubani, trust this stranger with her stories? How and why does Martine introduce Urmila as a character in this same story, as a Dalit midwife, the one Salhesh anoints as heir to the Sangha of Consciousness? How did a white woman and a Dalit woman come to think of themselves as sisters separated at birth?

Salhesh is the name for the unity between beings who don't often need language to express love. A triangle marked by a dot.

The story of Salhesh has been passed down for generations among the Dusadhs of Madhubani, a caste classified as Untouchable by hierarchy-loving Hindu Brahmanic codes, and as habitual criminals by the colonising British. In a stroke surpassing logic, the Dusadhs, who take pride in a history of military valour (like the Mahars do in western India), are characterized in versions of the Salhesh story as both the First Thief and the First Guard. In the conventional telling, Chuharmal is the thief, and

Salhesh the guard. In a landscape of such fictions that cannot overcome the tyrannies of caste, we have *The King of the Mountain*, where there are no villains. All are heroes. Chuharmal, Salhesh's cousin and rival who wills him to a war that Salhesh is loath to fight, is not cast as a villain in this telling. "The same consciousness in the goat and the hand that immolates it, in friend and foe. The same one also in Chuharmal and him." And yet, Dalit performances of the Salhesh and Chuharmal stories, considered subversive, have led to riots in Bihar in recent times.

The Dalit women of Madhubani continue to illustrate episodes of this epic. What does Salhesh look like? He is a triangle marked by a dot. Like the Bodhi tree, the open hand or the Wheel of Dhamma once sufficed to signify the Buddha. But the motif here is more abstract, geometric, bare, influenced as it is by godna/tattoo painting that the Dusadh women of Madhubani excel at, as well as by Vajrayana-laced Tantrism. An icon who is aniconic. A triangle marked by a dot is used to represent all men, women and gods, all becoming equal in art: Salhesh is mostly shown astride his similarly stylized elephant (Bhuranand in our story).

Our protagonist is Prince Jaybhardan, who wills himself to be reborn as an "Untouchable", so that he may one day become Salhesh and lead all humanity, indeed all sentient life, into a world where the binaries of high and low, of Brahmin and Chandala, of caste and outcaste will perish. How and why Salhesh appears to us like the historical Buddha, the mythical Shiva, one time as Rama, sometimes as Arjuna or Krishna, another time as Ashoka and even as Babasaheb Ambedkar is something that this outroduction will try to come to terms with.

▼

Madhubani lies by the foothills of the Himalayas in today's Bihar, a large state and much larger state of mind, that takes its name from the word vihara, a Buddhist place of dwelling and worship. Madhuban means the forest of honey; Madhubani means 'of the forest of honey'. The eponymous Madhubani paintings are from this land. In an earlier time, this cultural-geographic terrain was known as Mithila (whence its language Maithili). Sita, the tragic heroine of the epic *Ramayana*, was born here. A little further north is where Gotama Siddhartha was born, in Lumbini, in present-day Nepal. At some point in history, these lands were awash with ideas of equality, of the shattering of hierarchies, of nibbana or enlightenment being attainable in the here and now, not the hereafter. The stories of the *Mahabharata*, about the ruthless battle of Kurukshetra, where the song of *Gita* goads brother to kill brother, where five husbands mortgage one wife, and mother betrays son, also run their course through this land. This is the homeland of the Dusadh community (whose men often take the last name Paswan, like Urmila's husband), who today number about eight million people spread across northern and eastern India (Bihar, Jharkhand, Uttar Pradesh, Madhya Pradesh, Rajasthan, Delhi, West Bengal and Odisha) and Nepal, and the diaspora in Mauritius, Guyana and Suriname.

Seven rivers, big and small, including the mighty Ganga, ribbon their way through Madhubani. The saga of Salhesh bobs and weaves upon such unstill and unpredictable waters, across rivers that both brighten lives and sadden them with their floods and droughts, thrusting a contested history towards an impending future, fusing mythology with militant ideas of equality and justice.

Prince Jaybhardan is the eldest of the three sons of King Somdev, ruler of a small kingdom of Mahisautha, nestled in the Gangetic plains, swept by the humid winds of Bengal and kissed by the many moods of the Himalayas. Swollen with dreams, the rivers harass the land. Wanting to seduce and ravish the Mountain, they hoist themselves up to its belly. Here, we are told, the Mountain rises so prodigiously that even on the opposite end of the Earth, the soil was still Shiva's and none could prove that it otherwise. Yet this enchanted land, where nature is willing to share its magic with everyone, is blotted with discrimination. There is the horror of caste. There's Untouchability and there's the vile Brahmin who thinks that mere birth makes him virtuous and great. To Somdev's heir, the obligation of doing one's "caste duty" is anathema.

Once Jaybhardan becomes old enough to assume

the responsibilities of his rank, he is guided by his own internal light and refuses either to marry or to accept his role as heir to the throne. He chooses instead to re-implant himself in the form of an embryo in the womb of a pregnant woman from the humblest social status so as to be reborn as an Untouchable and begin his mission to bring peace to all humanity.

All wretched bounds must be crossed, all bonds broken to boundlessness; a great annihilation must ensue, but without violence, with only volition and consciousness, he resolves, leaving his teachers and peers in awe. Jaybhardan announces his decision to "go forth" and become the "thus-gone-one" or the Tathagata, as the Buddha was also known.

> The frustrated courtiers brooded, all the more bitterly in that Jaybhardan had started holding forth on "the necessity of educating children". Someone had even heard him talk of including the sons of mahouts and bricklayers—whom the knights called "the dregs of the earth".

In a deeply divided society, Jaybhardan's idea of unity is grand, and revolutionary. The crown prince is not keen to be king. He wishes to be the Emperor of all Consciousness and liberate humanity from both its thrall and will to power. A triangle haloed within the subtle throb of awareness.

To clarify the techne of such a telling involves revealing the telos. "Known by the name of Salhesh, 'King of the Mountain', his fame would extend to the farthest reaches of the inhabited Earth." And equally, it works the other way around: the end involves the means, an oral palimpsest being the natural state of all storytelling; author-ity a rather parochial literary dogma (that foils transcendence), a claim of patent based in property law. Let us remind ourselves that the Epic of Salhesh is to millions of Dalits what the *Mahabharata* and *Ramayana* and their allied lore are for most Hindus. It's a tale that has been told forever. But unlike the savarna Hindu instinct that feels compelled to confirm the historical veracity, and thus the supremacy, of its myths, Jaybhardan–Salhesh has one foot in history and one outside of it; he is a historical immortal. After all, Salhesh is after the conquest of the self and how this conquest can be made possible for all of humanity that knows only dukkha, suffering; the transcending of all boundaries between the self and the other, between the flower and the light that falls on it. He helps people ascend the nameless Mountain within, that is just as majestic and sublime as the external manifestation, the Himalayas. What is the Mountain, really? A triangle marked by a dot. It is Salhesh. The Salhesh within us.

▼

It is no coincidence that Salhesh often comes across sounding like the Buddha in many of his suttas or like Ambedkar in his political writings and speeches. When he speaks of the void as being the same as plenitude, Salhesh goes to the core of the Heart Sutra, which says emptiness is form and form is emptiness. This is the most frequently cited, recited, copied text in the Mahayana Buddhist tradition, and is also regarded as a Tantric text. The Mountain is the mind. A triangle marked by a dot.

Salhesh ushers in the Revolution of Love, a revolution that spreads far and wide. He speaks of sharing, of looks and gestures measured with respect, of simply paying attention. Above all: paying attention to other beings. As Martine, the midwife of this story, who in the course of paying attention to Urmila—to her drawings, to the movements of her brush, to her breath, to her being—can see Salhesh turn to Urmila for help.

Like Siddhartha, Jaybhardan is known for the "irresistible attraction he held over people of all ages and from all walks of life". Like Siddhartha, Jaybhardan humbles arrogant Brahmins in debates:

> "The vile and the dregs are of the same divine essence as gold, as are Brahmins and pigs, the lotus flower and the smelly mulch whence it grows," he declared to the Brahmin, who blanched in horror. "A royal womb and a lowly one are equal, I can assure you, and the experience of being born from them is the same. You teach Divine Oneness: observe that I believe in it absolutely."
>
> The Brahmin collected his thoughts, hesitated briefly, then bowed to Jaybhardan, not out of guile, but because his soul was moved.

This being a Dalit-held Dalit-led Dalit-told Dalit-heard story, Jaybhardan, as he evolves into Salhesh, comes at one point to be painted in a distinct Ambedkarite hue. He appears dressed in "a never-seen shade of blue, one that no monsoon could fade, nor even cow's urine". And a young woman, proud of her caste, says: "Beware repugnant indigo. The blue of the lower social classes..." Today, this colour is associated with Ambedkar, Buddha, and the Dalit movement. Indigo is derived from the Greek 'indikon', meaning 'from India'.

The story of Salhesh is inseparable from its modes of transmission. It is universal by not succumbing to the pressure of elitism and its narrow literary priorities. Universality here is resistance to elitism.

It is no coincidence that Salhesh sometimes reminds you of Ashoka the Great, who, after mongering war in his early years, embraced Buddhism, called himself Devanampiya or Beloved of the Gods, and carved out edicts that exhorted people to be kind towards all sentient beings. However, Salhesh comes to this conclusion without shedding any blood, without announcing himself with edicts. In declaring "I have faith in a general intuition", Salhesh even appears to paraphrase Marx's idea of "generic humanity". For Marx, in a communist society

> nobody has one exclusive sphere of activity but each can become accomplished in any branch he wishes, society regulates the general production and thus makes it possible

for me to do one thing today and another tomorrow, to hunt in the morning, fish in the afternoon, rear cattle in the evening, criticize after dinner, just as I have a mind, without ever becoming hunter, fisherman, herdsman or critic.

Salhesh's words, as presented in *The King of the Mountain*, echo also the ideas of Gorakhnath, the twelfth century anti-Brahmin Tantric mystic; they resonate with the weaver-poet Kabir's words from sixteenth-century Benares. In this timeless telling, then, no one historical or mythological allusion can bind Salhesh or wear him down. He is singular in his universality. If he appears like Siddhartha or Ambedkar, he is equally a devout worshipper of Durga and Shiva, and he prays to them to get out of sticky situations with magic and elan. The story of Salhesh is a story of no pure origins—just like Salhesh has no pure origins.

The King of the Mountain also features Shiva and Krishna as gods in heaven offering us an editorializing commentary, watching Jaybhardan become Salhesh. It is a battle of wits that Shiva seems to easily win, as he prides himself on his ward's doings:

> "After all, in essence, true consciousness is action."
> "Salhesh is building a sturdy base for the new society: moral education with a demanding awareness..."
> "Educating all those humans will wear Salhesh out."

This stands the philosophy of the *Bhagvad Gita* on its head. Here, consciousness is action; action cannot be a caste-bound duty, that may occasionally lead up to murder, as Krishna would have Arjuna (and us) believe. Ambedkar has remarked that the *Gita* offered "an unheard of defence of murder".

Salhesh has been avidly documented also by non-Dalit historians and colonial ethnographers. Sir George Grierson (1851–1941), the Irish linguist and civil servant, records for us "the song of King Salhes" as "taken down from the mouth of a Dom" (a cremation worker, considered the lowest of Untouchable castes), and speaks of how you can find a shrine (known locally as gahwar) for Salhesh under a pipal/bodhi tree in villages across five districts of the Tirhut region. In the past few decades, the hindutva machine has usurped these traditions, the groundwork for which was laid in the 1970s under Congress regimes, when, according to the scholar Badri Narayan, Brahmanical appropriation began with a slew of plays and novels based on the Salhesh story. A "Salhesh Section" was opened in Patna's state-run Vidyapati Bhavan. Efforts are on to enlist Salhesh to serve the cause of caste even when Salhesh is an anti-caste hero. Today, hindutva, the ideology of caste supremacism, has been actively rewriting the Salhesh story and presenting him as a version of the mythological king Rama. New scripts are being written and staged with fanfare. The small terracotta figures under banyan and pipal trees are making way for massive Salhesh temples.

The triangle marked by a dot is under siege.

However, Martine tells us in her Afterword that most historians and writers, even those that have done "fieldwork" among Dalits, as it is often thoughtlessly and brazenly called, have been unheeding of the one singular Dusadh version of the story that she heeds:

> A "new element" later emerged, which confirmed Salhesh's singularity: the Dusadh believe that although he belonged to the social class called kshatriya, comprising sovereigns and warriors, he chose to withdraw from it to become a poor man... The rebirth of Jaybhardan, heir to Somdev's throne, as an Untouchable was a major event—yet we found no trace of it among any of the historians we consulted. It's not actually all that surprising, though, since the Dusadh are considered Dalits, and their culture is essentially overlooked by Hindu society. Fortunately, Urmila Devi and her husband recounted the episode to us. She also illustrated it with great virtuosity.

Unlike the Buddha who needs to be convinced by his disciple Ananda about admitting women into the sangha, Salhesh is quick to insist on how the Revolution of Love cannot be complete without women. An onlooker heaps contempt on him: "First women, and now billy goats... His keeping company with the ugly and deformed, whose meals he agreed to share." Salhesh forms a new minority society with seven hundred men and seven hundred women who come from a cross-section of the *ancien régime*.

And unlike the Buddha and other serious men of history, Salhesh lacks sanctimony.

> He knew perfectly well that his teaching exhausted them, but he remained convinced it was his duty to massage their intelligence as a wet nurse massages a newborn's muscles. The words had to be repeated, over and over, so they would penetrate the scalp like oil, easing in here, caressing there, wrapped in a song that carried the message to the universe. Even if they didn't assimilate every single detail, it would do. What he had drummed into their heads would sprout and bloom. By the time he had finished, most of the women, and the men, had dozed off.

Here's greatness that makes you doze off—human, frail, fragile. Yet what such genius leaves behind is the prototype of a habitable, realizable society where there are no hierarchies. In Martine's telling, suffused by Urmila's vision, in order to achieve Original Unity, Salhesh is obliged to confront what he had overlooked until then—his feminine aspect and the magical forces that are none other than the profound forces of nature.

When Salhesh leaves it all behind and walks away, leaving a space at once empty and full of light, he passes the baton of consciousness to Urmila, to preside over a society where there would be no more castes or outcastes. Salhesh offers us what Ambedkar would theorize many centuries later—an Associated Life. A life of principles, not rules and rituals.

When we actually ascend a mountain, we reach a place where we forget the shape of the Mountain. We learn to disregard what it looks like, the representations and relations that grip it. And there it is. In the bottom of our heart. Everywhere.

Salhesh reverses the triangle.

S. Anand
14 April 2021
New Delhi

(Anand is publisher, Navayana)

Martine Le Coz is a novelist, poet and artist from Amboise, central France. Her historical novel *Céleste* won the Prix Renaudot in 2001. Her work with artists of the Mithila region since 2012 has led to three books: *Mithila, l'honneur des femmes (Mithila: Women's Honour*, 2013), *Les Filles de Krishna prennent la parole (Krishna's Daughters Speak Up,* 2016), and a set of oracle cards (drawings and texts) called *Sept Saris* (Seven Saris, 2018).

Regan Kramer is a bilingual and bicultural translator who divides her time between Paris and New York. Her translations include Olivier Bourdeaut's *Waiting for Bojangles* (2019), Jean-Gabriel Causse's *The Algorithm of the Heart* (2019), and François Zimeray's *I Saw Everywhere the Same Face* (2016).

Martine Le Coz
Photography: Dorothy Shoes